PEOPLE

LOVE

DEAD

JEWS

PEOPLE
LOVE
DEAD
JEWS

Reports from a Haunted Present

DARA HORN

W. W. NORTON & COMPANY
Independent Publishers Since 1923

Essays in this book originally appeared, in different form, in the following publications: "Everyone's (Second) Favorite Dead Jew" and "Dead Jews of the Desert" in *Smithsonian*; "Frozen Jews," "Fictional Dead Jews," and passages from "Executed Jews" in *Tablet*; "Dead American Jews, Part One" and "Dead American Jews, Part Two" in the *New York Times*; "Executed Jews" in *Jewish Review of Books*; "Legends of Dead Jews" in *Azure*, as well as in the anthology *Esther in America* (Stuart Halpern, ed., Maggid Books, 2021, reprinted with permission from Maggid Books); and "Blockbuster Dead Jews" in the *Atlantic*. "On Rescuing Jews and Others" was originally published by *Tablet* as an Amazon Kindle Single entitled *The Rescuer*.

For information about permission to reproduce selections from this book, write to Permissions, W. W. Norton & Company, Inc., 500 Fifth Avenue, New York, NY 10110

For information about special discounts for bulk purchases, please contact W. W. Norton Special Sales at specialsales@wwnorton.com or 800-233-4830

Manufacturing by LSC Communications, Harrisonburg
Production manager: Beth Steidle

Library of Congress Cataloging-in-Publication Data

Names: Horn, Dara, 1977– author.
Title: People love dead Jews : reports from a haunted present / Dara Horn.
Description: First edition. | New York : W. W. Norton & Company, 2021. |
Includes bibliographical references and index.
Identifiers: LCCN 2021012209 | ISBN 9780393531565 (hardcover) |
ISBN 9780393531572 (epub)
Subjects: LCSH: Jews—History. | Jews—Public opinion. |
Jews—Persecutions—Public opinion. | Antisemitism—History. |
Death—Political aspects. | Horn, Dara, 1977–
Classification: LCC DS117 .H66 2021 | DDC 909/.04924—dc23
LC record available at https://lccn.loc.gov/2021012209

W. W. Norton & Company, Inc., 500 Fifth Avenue, New York, N.Y. 10110
www.wwnorton.com

W. W. Norton & Company Ltd., 15 Carlisle Street, London W1D 3BS

1 2 3 4 5 6 7 8 9 0

For Maya, Ari, Eli, and Ronen,
who know how to live

CONTENTS

Introduction

IN THE

HAUNTED

PRESENT

SOMETIMES YOUR BODY IS SOMEONE ELSE'S HAUNTED house. Other people look at you and can only see the dead.

I first discovered this at the age of seventeen in the most trivial of moments, at an academic quiz bowl tournament in Nashville, Tennessee—where, as the only girl from my New Jersey high school, I shared a hotel room with two girls from Mississippi. We were strangers and competitors pretending to be friends. One night we stayed up late chatting about our favorite childhood TV shows, about how we had each believed that Mr. Rogers was personally addressing us through the screen. We laughed together until one girl said, "It's like Jesus. Even if he didn't know my name when he was dying on the cross, I still know he loved me, and if he knew my name, he would have loved me too." The other girl squealed, "I know, right? It's just like Jesus!" Then the two of them, full of messianic joy, looked at me.

I said nothing—a very loud nothing. The girls waited, uncomfortable, until one braved the silence. "It seems like people up north are much less religious," she tried. "How often do you go to church?"

It so happened that I was very religious. My family attended synagogue services weekly, or even more often than that; my parents were volunteer lay leaders in our congregation, and I had a job chanting publicly from the Torah scroll for the children's congregation every Saturday morning, which effectively meant that I knew large swaths of the Five Books of Moses in the original Hebrew by heart. On Sundays, I spent four hours learning ancient Jewish legal texts at a program for teenagers at a rabbinical school in New York, and from eight to ten p.m. every Tuesday and Thursday, I studied Hebrew language in a local adult-education class. My public school closed for Rosh Hashanah and Yom Kippur, but my siblings and I also skipped school for holidays like Sukkot, Simchat Torah, Passover, and Shavuot. I read works of Jewish philosophy for fun, tracking medieval and modern arguments about the nature of God. I often privately began and ended my days with traditional Hebrew prayers.

All of this and more required an enormous amount of countercultural effort, education, and commitment on the part of my family that vastly exceeded merely "going to church." But I sensed that this—"this" being the central pillar of my experience as a human being—was irrelevant to the question these girls were asking me. I mumbled something about a synagogue and tried to think of a way to steer us back to Mr. Rogers. But now the girls were staring at me, gaping in disbelief.

"You," one of the girls stammered, "you—you have blond hair!"

The second girl inspected me, squinting at my face in a way that made me wonder if I had acne. "And what color are your eyes?"

"Blue," I said.

The first girl said, "I thought Hitler said you all were dark."

In retrospect I can imagine many ways I might have felt about this statement, but at the time I was only baffled. I pictured my hand on the quiz-bowl buzzer I'd been pounding all week, and provided the correct answer: "Hitler was full of shit."

After a pause that lasted an eternity, one girl meekly offered, "I guess you're kind of right." *Kind of.* The other girl doubled down, demanding an explanation for my eye color if I were "from the Middle East." But I was done being nice, if being nice meant defending my own face. I left the room, confused.

That night I blurted to my mother from a hotel pay phone, "I don't get it. These girls made it to the nationals. These are the smart people! And they're getting their information from Hitler?"

My mother sighed, a long, tired sigh. "I know," she said, without elaborating. "I know."

My mother was the age then that I am now. And now I know too.

Those girls were not stupid, and probably not even bigoted. But in their entirely typical and well-intentioned education, they had learned about Jews mainly because people had killed Jews. Like most people in the world, they had only encountered dead Jews: people whose sole attribute was that they had been murdered, and whose murders served a clear purpose, which was *to teach us something.* Jews were people who, for moral and educational purposes, were supposed to be dead.

It took me many years to understand that those girls were not entirely wrong to look at me and think only of a terrifying past. I often felt haunted too.

When I was a child, I had a question that burned within me, and Judaism seemed to answer it. My question was about the nature of time.

I was obsessed with the unspoken and unnerving problem of being trapped in an eternal and inescapable present. As I got into bed each night, I would lie in the dark and wonder: *This day that just ended is gone now. Where did it go?* If I were a character in one of my novels, I would give the character a motivation for that constant longing. But I am not a fictional character. I had few words then for this deep sense of loss, nor any clear reason for it, other than that my mother came from a long line of women who had all died young, and her mourning for her own mother was something I observed and absorbed, without knowing what she or I was missing. The secondary nature of this grief only underscored the inexpressible feeling I had of arriving too late. With nothing to mourn, I nonetheless felt as though something were constantly flowing out of my life, just beneath its relentlessly cheerful surface. When I began writing as a child, my driving force was not the urge to invent stories but the urge to stop time, to preserve those disappearing days. I kept journals that were more like reporter's notebooks, taking minutes on even the most boring events for no reason other than to lock them down on paper. It did not occur to me that most people were not concerned with this problem. It did not occur to me because in my family's religious practice, I found many thousands of years' worth of people who shared my obsession with this problem—and who had, to my child's mind, succeeded in solving it.

One of America's many foundational legends is that it doesn't matter who your parents are, or who their parents were, or where you came from—that what matters is what you do now with the opportunities this country presents to you, and this is what we call the American dream. The fact that this legend is largely untrue does not detract from its power; legends are not reports on reality but expressions of a culture's values and aspirations. Judaism, too, has many foundational legends, and all of them express exactly the opposite of this idea. Ancient rabbinic tradition insists that it was not merely our ancestors who were liberated from Egyptian slavery, but that *we ourselves* were also personally freed by God. When God gave the Israelites the laws of the Torah at Mount Sinai, this tradition teaches, it was not merely that generation of Israelites who were present, but all of their future descendants—both biological and spiritual—stood with them at Sinai. In America, time was supposed to be a straight line where only the future mattered; in Judaism, it was more like a spiral of a spiral, a tangled old telephone cord in which the future was the present, which was essentially the past.

This profound difference between these two sides of my identity was not abstract or subtle; it was obvious even to a child. In public school, my classmates and I pledged allegiance to the flag and aspired to form a more perfect union, fully invested in America's future. But when we learned about the past—Pilgrims and Native Americans, Patriots and Tories, Yankees and Rebels—there was no "we." In Hebrew school and in the traditional texts I read in synagogue and at home, it was just the opposite. The Hebrew Bible was never discussed in historical context, because we were the historical context. It was our present, and in my family's religious life, it was treated that way. The creation of the world recurred every week at our Sabbath table, where we chanted Hebrew biblical passages about God resting on the seventh day and sang long medieval Hebrew poems about divine creativity in multipart harmony. On Passover, we ate the same matzah we'd been eating for millennia, still unable to find the time to let our bread rise during our flight to freedom. Every New Year, Abraham once more drew his knife to his son Isaac's throat, holding our future hostage, fate and free will bound together in a double helix that caught us in its grip.

When I went to Israel for the first time at the age of nine, I was stunned to discover that there was an actual answer to my question about where those disappearing days had gone: they were underground. The first time I entered Jerusalem's Old City, I walked down a flight of stairs that began on the current street level; at the bottom, I was stunned to step onto the paving stones from the street level during the Roman period, as though I had traveled through time instead of rock. The city itself was a kind of *tel*, an archaeological mound with layers of past centuries piled one on the other, some of which were preserved and exposed. As I grew older, I discovered that people had these layers too—that all people had those vanished days within them, whether or not they knew it. There was an alternative to being trapped in the present: a deep consciousness of memory that transcended any one person or lifetime. I dove into this possibility, body and soul. My studies of Hebrew—the language itself had layers, from airheaded TV shows all the way down to biblical bedrock—led to studies of Yiddish, which led to a doctorate in both, which flowed into my fiction. I wrote my way down into that tunnel through time, burrowing deeper into a past that was in fact the present, a breathing reality just beneath the surface of the current moment, until I was no longer afraid to fall asleep.

This, to me, was what being Jewish meant, the gift it gave me in the wonderland of a country that long ago gave my family a future. But as I slowly came to understand, this was not what it meant to people who weren't Jewish, or even to many Jews with little education in the culture. What Jewish identity meant to those people, it turned out, was simply a state of nonbeing: not being Christian or Muslim or whatever else other people apparently were (in Britain, for instance, more people identify as Jedis than as Jews), being alienated, being marginalized, or best of all, being dead. As thousands of Holocaust books and movies and TV shows and lectures and courses and museums and mandatory school curricula made abundantly clear, dead Jews were the most popular of all.

For most of my adult life, I had no reason to recall that moment in the Nashville hotel. I had filed it deep in my brain, in the same mental sock drawer where I kept the high schoolers from the adjacent town who cheered for my school's soccer team to "go to the gas," or the student in the first college class I ever taught who refused to read an assigned 1933 Hebrew novel because Hebrew was "racist," or the roommate who sobbed uncontrollably while informing me that I was going to hell. (I reassured her that at least I would know a lot of people there.) These incidents were oddities, weird and even laughable. They weren't my normal, or the normal of anyone I knew.

More than twenty-five years later, they still aren't my normal, though they are now the normal of more than a few people I know. But in recent years I have had the misfortune of discovering the deep vein of normalcy that runs beneath these oddities, which is shared by seemingly good-faith cultural enterprises like Holocaust museums, canonical Western literature, and the elaborate restoration of Jewish historical sites as far away as China. I began to notice a certain gaslighting about the Jewish past and present that I had never seen before, even when it was right in front of me. I had mistaken the enormous public interest in past Jewish suffering for a sign of respect for living Jews. I was very wrong.

This fact should have been obvious to me from the beginning of my writing career, when my most acclaimed early published piece, the one nominated for a major award, wasn't the one about Jewish historical sites in Spain but rather the one about death camps. I made a point of resisting this reality, asking people at my public talks if they could name three death camps, and then asking the same people if they could name three Yiddish authors—the language spoken by over 80 percent of death-camp victims. What, I asked, was the point of caring so much about how people died, if one cared so little about how they lived? At the time, I did not appreciate how deep the obsession with dead Jews went, how necessary it was to so many people's unarticulated concept of civilization, to their unarticulated concept of themselves. But as our current century wore on and public conversations about Israel became increasingly toxic—far beyond any normal political concern—and as public conversations about observant Jews took on the same tone, I came to recognize the mania for dead Jews as something deeply perverse, and all the more so when it wore its goodwill on its sleeve. I dealt with this perversity in the most honorable way possible: by avoiding it.

For a writer and scholar of Jewish history and literature, this was challenging, because it meant avoiding the subjects my readers and students clearly loved most. Still, I tried. I wrote novels about Jewish spies during the Civil War, about a medieval Hebrew archive in Cairo, about Soviet Yiddish Surrealists, about a woman born in ancient Jerusalem who couldn't manage to die. In my university courses and lectures, I emphasized the unprecedented revival of Hebrew, the evolving patterns of Israeli fiction, the growth of modern Yiddish poetry and drama out of traditional art forms, the complex internal religious debates that shaped secular writers' works generations later. I fought hard to keep everything as autonomous as possible, making sure to tell the stories of how Jews had lived and what they had lived for, rather than how they had died. As I insisted to my Nashville roommates long ago, I was not that dark.

But the past kept seeping into the present. By the end of 2018, after a massacre of Jews in our more perfect union that hardly came from nowhere, the only thing my readers, students, colleagues, and editors wanted me to talk about was dead Jews. I became the go-to person for the emerging literary genre of synagogue-shooting op-eds—a job I did not apply for, but one that I accepted out of fear of what someone less aware of history might write instead. Even outside of those news-headline incidents, I found myself asked, again and again, for my opinions on dead Jews. Perhaps I was expected to approach the subject with a kind of piety, an attitude that would generate some desperately needed hope and grace. After all, I was a living Jew (a writer, a religious person, even a Hebrew and Yiddish scholar), so I was clearly equipped to say something decorous and inspiring, something sad and beautiful that would flatter everyone involved.

I couldn't do it. I was too angry. My children were growing up in an America very different from the one I'd grown up in, one where battling strangers' idiocies consumed large chunks of brain space and where the harassment and gaslighting of others—encounters like those I'd once buried in my mental sock drawer—were not the exception but the rule. My efforts to prove a negative—that we weren't all dark—had failed, overwhelmed by the reality of being part of a ridiculously small minority that nonetheless played a behemoth role in other people's imaginations.

So instead of avoiding and rejecting this haunted-house world, where my family's identity was defined and determined by the opinions and projections of others, I decided to lean directly into that distorted public looking glass and report what I found there: to unravel, document, describe, and artic- ulate the endless unspoken ways in which the popular obses- sion with dead Jews, even in its most apparently benign and civic-minded forms, is a profound affront to human dignity. I wish I did not feel the need to do this. But I want my children, and your children, to know.

This book explores the many strange and sickening ways in which the world's affection for dead Jews shapes the present moment. I hope you will find it as disturbing as I do.

December 2020

PEOPLE

LOVE

DEAD

JEWS

Chapter 1

EVERYONE'S
(SECOND) FAVORITE
DEAD JEW

PEOPLE LOVE DEAD JEWS. LIVING JEWS, NOT SO MUCH.

This disturbing idea was suggested by an incident in 2018 at the Anne Frank House, the blockbuster Amsterdam museum built out of Frank's "Secret Annex," or in Dutch, "Het Achter-huis [The House Behind]"—a series of tiny hidden rooms where the teenage Jewish diarist lived with her parents, her sister, and four other persecuted Jews for over two years before being captured by Nazis and deported to Auschwitz in 1944. Here's how much people love dead Jews: Anne Frank's diary, first published in Dutch in 1947 via her surviving father, Otto Frank, has been translated into seventy languages and has sold more than 30 million copies worldwide, and the Anne Frank House now hosts well over a million visitors each year, with reserved tickets selling out months in advance. But when a young employee at the Anne Frank House tried to wear his yarmulke to work, his employers told him to hide it under a baseball cap. The museum's goal was "neutrality," one spokesperson explained to the British newspaper *Daily Mail*, and a live Jew in a yarmulke might "interfere" with the museum's "independent position." The museum finally relented after deliberating for four months, which seems like a rather long time for the Anne Frank House to ponder whether it was a good idea to force a Jew into hiding.

One could call this a simple mistake, except that it echoed a similar incident the previous year, when visitors noticed a discrepancy in the museum's audio-guide displays. Each audio-guide language was represented by a national flag—with the exception of Hebrew, which was represented only by the language's name in its alphabet. The display was eventually corrected to include the Israeli flag.

These public-relations mishaps, clumsy though they may have been, were not really mistakes, nor were they even the fault of the museum alone. On the contrary: these instances of concealed Jewish identity are the key to the runaway success of Anne Frank's diary and fame. This sort of hiding was an essential part of the diary's original publication, in which several direct references to Jewish practice were edited away. They were also part of the psychological legacy of Anne Frank's parents and grandparents, German Jews for whom the price of admission to Western society was assimilation, hiding their differences by accommodating and ingratiating themselves to the culture that ultimately sought to destroy them. That price lies at the heart of Anne Frank's endless appeal. After all, Anne Frank had to hide her identity so much that she was forced to spend two years in a closet rather than breathe in public. And that closet, hiding place for a dead Jewish girl, is what millions of visitors want to see.

———————

Surely there is nothing left to say about Anne Frank, except that there is everything left to say about her: all the books she never lived to write. For she was unquestionably a talented writer, possessed of both the ability and the commitment that real literature requires. Quite the opposite of how the influential Dutch historian Jan Romein described her work in April of 1946, in his article in the newspaper *Het Parool* that spurred her diary's publication—a "diary by a child, this *de profundis* stammered out in a child's voice"— Frank's diary was not the work of a naif, but rather of a writer already planning future publication. Frank had begun the diary casually, but soon sensed its potential. Upon hearing a radio broadcast in March of 1944 calling on Dutch civilians to preserve diaries and other personal wartime documents, she immediately began to revise two years of previous entries, with a title (*Het Achterhuis*, or *The House Behind*) already in mind, along with pseudonyms for the hiding place's residents. Nor were her revisions simple corrections or substitutions. They were thoughtful edits designed to draw the reader in, intentional and sophisticated. Her first entry in the original diary, for instance, begins with a long description of her birthday gifts (the blank diary being one of them), an entirely unself-conscious record by a thirteen-year-old girl. The first entry in her revised version, on the other hand, begins with a deeply self-aware and ironic pose: "It's an odd idea for someone like me to keep a diary; not only because I have never done so before, but because it seems to me that neither I—nor for that matter anyone else—will be interested in the unbosomings of a thirteen-year-old schoolgirl."

The innocence here is all affect, carefully achieved. Imagine writing this as your second draft, with a clear vision of a published manuscript; this is hardly the mind of a "stammering" child. In addition to the diary, Frank also worked hard on her stories, or as she proudly put it, "my pen-children are piling up." Some of these were scenes from her life in hiding, but others were entirely invented: stories of a poor girl with six siblings, or a dead grandmother protecting her orphaned grandchild, or a novel-in-progress about star-crossed lovers featuring multiple marriages, depression, a suicide, and prophetic dreams. Already wary of a writer's pitfalls, she noted, "It isn't sentimental nonsense for it's modeled on the story of Daddy's life."

"I am the best and sharpest critic of my own work," she wrote a few months before her arrest. "I know myself what is and what is not well written."

What is and what is not well written: it is likely that Frank's opinions on this subject would have evolved if she had had the opportunity to age. Reading the diary as an adult, one sees the limitations of a teenager's perspective, and longs for more. In one entry, Frank describes how her father's business partners—now her family's protectors—hold a critical corporate meeting in the office below the family's hiding place. Her father, she, and her sister discover that they can hear what is said by lying down with their ears pressed to the floor. In Frank's telling, the episode is a comic one; she gets so bored that she falls asleep. But adult readers cannot help but ache for her father, a man who clawed his way out of bankruptcy to build a business now stolen from him, reduced to lying facedown on the floor just to overhear what his subordinates might do with his life's work. When Frank complains about her insufferable middle-aged roommate Fritz Pfeffer (Albert Dussel, per Frank's pseudonym) taking his time on the toilet, adult readers might empathize with him as the only single adult in the group, permanently separated from his non-Jewish life partner whom he could not marry due to antisemitic laws. Readers Frank's age connect with her budding romance with fellow hidden resident Peter van Pels (renamed Peter van Daan), but adults might wonder how either of the married couples in the hiding place managed their own relationships in confinement with their children. More broadly, readers Frank's age relate to her constant complaints about grown-ups and their pettiness, but adults are equipped to appreciate these grown-ups' psychological devastation, how they endured not only their physical deprivation, but the greater blow of being reduced to a childlike state of dependence on the whims of others.

Frank herself sensed the limits of the adults around her, writing critically of her own mother's and Peter's mother's apparently trivial preoccupations—and in fact these women's circumstances, not only their wartime deprivation but their prewar lives as housewives, were a chief driver for Frank's ambitions. "I can't imagine that I would have to lead the same sort of life as Mummy and Mrs. v.P. [van Pels] and all the women who do their work and are then forgotten," she wrote. "I must have something besides a husband and children, something that I can devote myself to!" In the published diary, this passage is immediately followed by the famous words, "I want to go on living even after my death!"

By plastering this sentence on Frank's book jackets, publishers have implied that through her posthumous fame, the writer's dreams were achieved. But when we consider the writer's actual ambitions, it is obvious that her dreams were in fact destroyed—and that the writer who would have emerged from Frank's experience would not be anything like the writer Frank herself originally planned to become. Imagine this obituary of a life unlived:

> Anne Frank, noted Dutch novelist and essayist, died this past Wednesday at her home in Amsterdam. She was 92.
>
> A survivor of Auschwitz and Bergen-Belsen, Frank's acclaim was hard-won. In her twenties, Frank struggled to find a publisher for her first book, The House Behind, a memoir of her experiences in hiding and in Nazi concentration camps. Disfigured by a brutal beating, Frank rarely granted interviews; her later work, The Return, describes how her father did not recognize her upon their reunion in 1945.

Frank supported herself as a journalist, and in 1961 she earned notoriety for her fierce reporting on the Israeli capture of Nazi henchman Adolf Eichmann, an extradition via kidnapping that the European elite condemned. After covering Eichmann's Jerusalem trial for the Dutch press, Frank found the traction to publish Margot, *a novel that imagined her sister living the life she once dreamed of, as a midwife in the Galilee. A surreal work that breaks the boundaries between novel and memoir, and leaves ambiguous which of its characters are dead or alive, the Hebrew translation of* Margot *became a runaway bestseller, while an English-language edition eventually found a small but appreciative audience in the United States.*

Frank's subsequent books and essays brought her renown as a clear-eyed prophet carefully attuned to hypocrisy. Her reputation for relentless conscience, built on her many investigative articles on subjects ranging from Soviet oppression to Arab-Israeli wars, was cemented by her internationally acclaimed 1984 book Every House Behind, *written after her father's death. Beginning with an homage to her father's unconditional devotion, the book progresses into a searing and accusatory work that reimagines her childhood hiding place as a metaphor for Western civilization, whose façade of high culture concealed a demonic evil. "Every flat, every house, every office building in every city," she wrote, "they all have a House Behind."*

Her readers will long remember the words from her first book, quoted from a diary she kept at 15: "I don't believe that the big men are guilty of the war, oh no, the little man is just as guilty, otherwise the peoples of the world would have risen in revolt long ago! There's in people simply an urge to destroy, an urge to kill, to murder and rage, and until all mankind without exception undergoes a great change, wars will be waged, everything that has been built up, cultivated and grown will be cut down and disfigured, and mankind will have to begin all over again."

Her last book, a memoir, was titled To Begin Again.

The problem with this hypothetical, or any other hypothetical, about Frank's nonexistent adulthood isn't just the impossibility of knowing how Frank's life and career might have developed. The problem is that the entire appeal of Anne Frank to the wider world—as opposed to those who knew and loved her—lay in her lack of a future.

There is an exculpatory ease to embracing this "young girl," whose murder is almost as convenient for her many enthusiastic readers as it was for her persecutors, who found unarmed Jewish children easier to kill off than the Allied infantry. After all, an Anne Frank who lived might have been a bit upset at her Dutch betrayers, still unidentified, who received a reward for each Jew they turned in of approximately $1.40. An Anne Frank who lived might not have wanted to represent "the children of the world"—particularly since so much of her diary is preoccupied with a desperate plea to be taken seriously, to not be perceived as a child. Most of all, an Anne Frank who lived might have told people about what she saw at Westerbork, Auschwitz, and Bergen-Belsen, and people might not have liked what she had to say.

And here is the most devastating fact of Frank's posthumous success, which leaves her real experience forever hidden: we know what she would have said, because other people have said it, and we don't want to hear it.

The line most often quoted from Frank's diary are her famous words, "I still believe, in spite of everything, that people are truly good at heart." These words are "inspiring," by which we mean that they flatter us. They make us feel forgiven for those lapses of our civilization that allow for piles of murdered girls—and if those words came from a murdered girl, well, then, we must be absolved, because they must be true. That gift of grace and absolution from a murdered Jew (exactly the gift that lies at the heart of Christianity) is what millions of people are so eager to find in Frank's hiding place, in her writings, in her "legacy." It is far more gratifying to believe that an innocent dead girl has offered us grace than to recognize the obvious: Frank wrote about people being "truly good at heart" before meeting people who weren't. Three weeks after writing those words, she met people who weren't.

Here's how much some people dislike living Jews: they murdered 6 million of them. This fact bears repeating, as it does not come up at all in Anne Frank's writings. Readers of her diary are aware that the author was murdered in a genocide, but this does not mean that her diary is a work about genocide. If it were, it is unlikely that it would have been any-where near as universally embraced.

We know this, because there is no shortage of writings from victims and survivors who chronicled this fact in vivid detail, and none of those documents have achieved anything like Frank's diary's fame. Those that have come close have only done so by observing those same rules of hiding, the ones that insist on polite victims who don't insult their persecu-tors. The work that came closest to achieving Frank's interna-tional fame might be Elie Wiesel's *Night*, a memoir that could be thought of as a continuation of Frank's diary, recounting the tortures of a fifteen-year-old imprisoned in Auschwitz. As the scholar Naomi Seidman has discussed, Wiesel first pub-lished his memoir in Yiddish, under the title *And the World Was Silent*. The Yiddish book told the same story told in *Night*, but it exploded with rage against his family's murderers and, as the title implies, the entire world whose indifference (or active hatred) made those murders possible. With the help of the French Catholic Nobel laureate François Mauriac, Wie-sel later published a French version under the new title *La Nuit*—a work that repositioned the young survivor's rage into theological angst. After all, what reader would want to hear about how his society had failed, how he was guilty? Better to blame God. This approach earned Wiesel a Nobel Peace Prize, as well as, years later, selection for Oprah's Book Club, the American epitome of grace. It did not, however, make teen-age girls read his book in Japan, the way they read Frank's. For that he would have had to hide much, much more.

What would it mean for a writer not to hide this horror? There is no mystery here, only a lack of interest. You have probably never heard of another young murdered Jewish chronicler of the same moment, Zalmen Gradowski. Like Frank's, Gradowski's work was written under duress, and discovered only after his death—except that Gradowski's work was written in Auschwitz.

Gradowski, a young married man whose entire family was murdered, was one of the Jewish prisoners in Auschwitz's Sonderkommando: those forced to escort new arrivals into the gas chambers, haul the newly dead bodies to the crematoria, extract any gold teeth, and then burn them. He reportedly maintained his religious faith, reciting the Kaddish (mourner's prayer) each evening for the souls of the thousands of people whose bodies he burned that day— including Peter van Pels's father, who was gassed upon the group's arrival in Auschwitz on September 6, 1944. Gradowski recorded his experiences in Yiddish and buried the documents, which were discovered after the war; he himself was killed on October 7, 1944, in a Sonderkommando revolt he had organized that lasted only one day.

"I don't want to have lived for nothing like most people," Frank wrote in her diary. "I want to be useful or give pleasure to the people around me who don't yet know me, I want to go on living even after my death!" Gradowski, too, wrote with a purpose. But Gradowski's goal wasn't personal or public fulfillment. His was truth: searing, blinding prophecy, Jeremiah lamenting a world aflame.

"It may be that these, the lines that I am now writing, will be the sole witness to what was my life," Gradowski writes.

"But I shall be happy if only my writings should reach you, citizen of the free world. Perhaps a spark of my inner fire will ignite within you, and even should you sense only part of what we lived for, you will be compelled to avenge us—avenge our deaths! Dear discoverer of these writings! I have a request for you: this is the real reason why I write, that my doomed life may attain some meaning, that my hellish days and hopeless tomorrows may find a purpose in the future." And then Gradowski tells us what he has seen.

Gradowski's chronicle walks us, step by devastating step, through the murders of five thousand people, a single large "transport" of Czech Jews who were slaughtered on the night of March 8, 1944—a group that was unusual only because they had already been detained in Auschwitz for months, and therefore knew what was coming. Gradowski tells us how he escorted the thousands of women and young children into the disrobing room, marveling at how "these same women who now pulsed with life would lie in dirt and filth, their pure bodies smeared with human excrement." He describes how the mothers kiss their children's limbs, how sisters clutch each other, how one woman asks him, "Say, brother, how long does it take to die? Is it easy or hard?" Once the women are naked, Gradowski and his fellow prisoners escort them through a gauntlet of SS officers who had gathered for this special occasion—a night gassing arranged intentionally on the eve of Purim, the biblical festival celebrating the Jews' narrow escape from a planned genocide. He recalls how one woman, "a lovely blond girl," stopped in her death march to address the officers: "'Wretched murderers! You look at me with your thirsty, bestial eyes. You glut yourselves on my nakedness. Yes, this is what you've been waiting for. In your civilian lives you could never even have dreamed about it. [. . .] But you won't enjoy this for long. Your game's almost over, you can't kill all the Jews. And you will pay for it all.' And suddenly she leaped at them and struck Oberscharfuhrer Voss, the director of the crematoria, three times. Clubs came down on her head and shoulders. She entered the bunker with her head covered with wounds [. . .] she laughed for joy and proceeded calmly to her death." Gradowski describes how people sang in the gas chambers, songs that included "Hatikvah" (The Hope), now the national anthem of Israel. And then he describes the mountain of open-eyed naked bodies that he and his fellow prisoners had to pull apart and burn: "Their gazes were fixed, their bodies motionless. In the deadened, stagnant stillness there was only a hushed, barely audible noise—a sound of fluid seeping from the different orifices of the dead. [. . .] Frequently one recognizes an acquaintance." In the specially constructed ovens, he tells us, the hair is first to catch fire, but "the head takes the longest to burn; two little blue flames flicker from the eyeholes—these are the eyes burning with the brain. [. . .] The entire process lasts twenty minutes—and a human being, a world, has been turned to ashes. [. . .] It won't be long before the five thousand people, the five thousand worlds, will have been devoured by the flames."

Gradowski was not poetic; he was prophetic. He did not gaze into this inferno and ask why. He knew. Aware of both the long recurring arc of destruction in Jewish history, and of the universal fact of cruelty's origins in feelings of worthlessness, he writes: "This fire was ignited long ago by the barbarians and murderers of the world, who had hoped to drive darkness from their brutal lives with its light."

One can only hope that we have the courage to hear this truth without hiding, to face the fire and to begin again.

Chapter 2

FROZEN
JEWS

ONE OF MY STRANGE AND VIVID MEMORIES FROM MY first trip to Israel, when I was nine years old, is of a brief cartoon I watched at the Diaspora Museum in Tel Aviv. The cartoon described the travels of Benjamin of Tudela, a twelfth-century Spanish Jewish merchant who documented his six-year journey traversing the known world, across the Mediterranean to Turkey, Israel, Egypt, Babylonia, and Persia, and reporting on India and China, staying with Jewish communities in each place and sharing crowded boats and wagons in between. The Diaspora Museum has since been revamped and rebranded as the Museum of the Jewish People, but in 1986 it was a dark and openly depressing place, its dour displays about Jewish communities around the world all leading to a "Scrolls of Fire" atrium describing how the hapless Jews in these communities were either expelled or burned alive.

But the cartoon was bright and curious. Benjamin was a ridiculous bowling-pin figure with googly eyes, bobbing across the screen and cheerfully reporting on thriving Jewish communities around the world—the Jews in France who inexplicably lived in a castle, the Jews in Babylonia who had their own googly-eyed king, the Jews in Yemen who joined local Arab armies and stampeded with them in a cloud of dust, the Jews in Syria who pacified wiggly-eyebrowed assassins by offering free silk scarves. For reasons I could not articulate at the age of nine, I was utterly enchanted.

I feel that same enchantment now when I am seduced by the travel industry's branding of the world as an amazing place full of welcoming people who, beneath it all, are actually the same. In reality, the more time I have spent in any of the fifty-plus countries I have visited as a tourist, the more I notice the differences between myself and the inhabitants, and the more alienated, uncomfortable, and anxious I become. Yet colorful photos of exotic places on TripAdvisor lure me every time.

So I was eager to make my way to a city called Harbin in a remote province of northeastern China, south of Siberia and north of North Korea, where the temperature hovers around minus 35 Celsius for much of the year, and where every winter, over ten thousand workers construct an entire massive city out of blocks of ice. The Harbin Ice Festival dwarfs similar displays in Canada and Japan by orders of magnitude, its enormous ice buildings laced through with LED lighting and sometimes replicating famous monuments at or near life-size. It attracts over 2 million visitors a year; it needs to be seen to be believed. As I considered a trip to Harbin, my mindless travel-industry scrolling took me to a list of other local tourist attractions, including synagogues.

Yes, synagogues. Plural. And then I discovered something deeply strange: the city of Harbin was built by Jews.

———

Jews have lived in China for more than a thousand years, which is as long as they have lived in Poland. But the story of the Jews of Harbin, and of Harbin itself, begins with the railroad—because before the railroad, Harbin did not exist.

Like most Chinese cities you've never heard of, Harbin today is larger than New York, with a population around 16 million. But as late as 1896, there was only a cluster of small fishing villages around a bend in a river. That year Russia received a concession from China to build part of the Trans-Siberian Railroad through Manchuria—the traditional name for the vast, frigid, and, at that time, barely populated region of northeastern China. Building this route would shave precious time off the trip from Moscow to Vladivostok. The route would also include a branch line deeper into China, requiring a large administrative center at the junction—essentially, a town. Mikhail Gruliov, a Jew who had converted to Russian Orthodoxy in order to become a general in the Russian Army, selected the site that became Harbin.

With an enormous investment to protect, railroad officials quickly realized that they could not depend on local warlords or Siberian peasants to create this not-yet-existent town. They needed experienced Russian-speaking entrepreneurs. But who would ever want to move to Manchuria? The Russian minister of finance, Sergei Yulyevich Witte, hit on a genius idea: the Jews.

Russia's crippling antisemitic laws and violent pogroms were already driving hundreds of thousands of Jews to America, including my own ancestors. Witte argued to the regime in St. Petersburg that to get capital and talent to Manchuria, one only had to tell the Jews that they could live free of antisemitic restrictions—without learning a new language or becoming bottom-feeders in New York's sweatshops—if they moved there.

The regime reluctantly agreed. So did hundreds, and then thousands, of Russian Jews.

The first Jews arrived in 1898 and incorporated an official community in 1903; in only five years, the plan was working splendidly. A 1904 *National Geographic* article written by a U.S. consul to Manchuria reported, wide-eyed, that "one of the greatest achievements in city construction that the world has ever witnessed is now going on in the heart of Manchuria," and that "the capital for most of the private enterprises is furnished by Siberian Jews." These Jewish entrepreneurs created Harbin's first hotels, banks, pharmacies, insurance companies, department stores, publishing houses, and more. By 1909, twelve of the forty members of Harbin's city council were Jewish. These initial entrepreneurs were later joined by new Jewish veterans of the 1904–1905 Russo-Japanese War, then by Jewish refugees fleeing the 1905 Russian pogroms, then by even more refugees fleeing World War I and the Russian Civil War.

At its peak, Harbin's Jewish community numbered around

twenty thousand. The "Old" Synagogue was built in 1909, and by 1921 there was enough demand for a "New" Synagogue a few blocks away, as well as a kosher slaughterer, ritual bath, and matzah bakery, not to mention a Jewish elementary and secondary school, a hospital, a charity kitchen, a free loan association, an old-age home, multiple magazines and newspapers, performances of Jewish music and theater, and Zionist clubs that were the center of many young people's lives—featuring not only competitive athletics (these clubs owned their own sports facilities and even yachts) but also rigorous study of Hebrew language and Zionist ideas. Harbin hosted major international Zionist conferences that drew Jews from all over Asia. Zionist parades were held in the streets.

You already know this story has to end badly. Like almost every place Jews have ever lived, Harbin was great for the Jews until it wasn't—but in Harbin, the usual centuries-long rise-and-fall was condensed into approximately thirty years. The flood of refugees from the 1917 Russian Revolution included many non-Jewish "White" Russians (anti-Communist royalists), whose virulent antisemitism was soon institutionalized in a Fascist party within Harbin's government, and who burned the Old Synagogue in 1931. That was also the year the Japanese occupied Manchuria, noticed rich Jews there, and decided they wanted their money. Conveniently, White Russian thugs were ready to help.

The Japanese gendarmerie embarked on a partnership with White Russian criminals, targeting Jewish business owners and their families for extortion, confiscation, kidnapping, and murder. Later they manipulated the Jewish community for political purposes, sending Abraham Kaufman, a respected physician and the community's elected leader, off to two separate audiences with the Japanese emperor, and forcing him to publish official statements from Harbin's Jewish community announcing their love for Nazi-allied Japan. When the Soviets took over in 1945, they rounded up the city's remaining Jewish leaders, including Dr. Kaufman, and sent them to gulags. Dr. Kaufman endured eleven years in a gulag and then five years in exile in Kazakhstan before he was allowed to join his family in Israel. He was the luckiest; no one else survived. Then again, dying in a gulag was less dramatic than the fate of some Jews under the Japanese. While retreating from the Manchurian town of Hailar, the Japanese military beheaded its Jewish residents.

By 1949, Chinese Maoists controlled Harbin. The thousand-plus Jews still in town were gradually stripped of their businesses and livelihoods, while Israel's government made secret contact with Harbin's remaining Jews and began arranging for them to leave—a process that mostly involved submitting to extortion. As Walter Citrin, an Israeli official responsible for facilitating Jewish emigration from Communist China, explained, "It is obvious that the Communist government is keen to clear the country of the foreign element. However . . . the authorities make things very difficult as long as the person who wants to leave is still in funds, and let the person go only after making quite sure that his personal funds are exhausted." The last Jewish family left town in 1962. After that, only one Jew remained in the city, a woman named Hannah Agre, who refused to leave. Leaning into the crazy-old-lady motif, she moved into a tiny room in the Old Synagogue (by then the building, its interior subdivided, was being used as government office space) and died there in 1985, the official Last Jew of Harbin.

She wasn't quite the last, though. Today there is one Jew in Harbin, an Israeli in his seventies named Dan Ben-Canaan. Ben-Canaan was covering the Far East for Israeli news media when he was invited to teach at a local university, and he settled permanently in Harbin in 2002. Ben-Canaan is a busy man, not only because of his university responsibilities and his work editing local English-language news programs, but because his enormous research into Harbin's Jewish past has made him indispensable to the local government as they restore Jewish sites—so he is also basically employed as the semiofficial One Jew of Harbin.

Ben-Canaan spends enough of his time being the One Jew of Harbin that when I first spoke with him over Skype, he had his one-liner ready: "I'm the president of the community here, which consists of me and me alone. It's great because I don't have anyone to argue with." Ben-Canaan's interest in Harbin's Jewish history, stemming from his days as a journalist, intensified when he learned that Harbin's government owned the Jewish community's official archives—and kept them under lock and key. "I tried to get them to reopen the archives, and they refused," he told me. "I've been given two reasons for it. One is that it contains politically sensitive material, and the other is that they're afraid of being sued for property restitution. There were some wealthy Jews here whose property was worth millions." The lack of access motivated Ben-Canaan to re-create the archives himself by collecting photographs, memorabilia, and testimony from more than eight hundred former Harbin Jews and their descendants around the world. As a result, as he put it, "I've become an address" for Harbin's Jewish history. When the provincial government decided—for reasons that only gradually became clear to me—to spend $30 million to restore, renovate, or reconstruct its synagogues and other Jewish buildings, they hired him.

The One Jew of Harbin spoke with me for nearly two hours, because that was how long it took him to describe the Jewish sites whose refurbishment he had supervised. There was apparently a lot to see. When I asked if I might meet him in Harbin in January, he laughed, explaining that he spends his winters in southern China. "Winter here is not like winter in other places," he warned me. "You can't just walk around outside. Come in the spring or summer instead." But I'd been lured by the city of ice. So he connected me with one of his former students who now worked as a tour guide, and I was on my way.

———

There is a tourist-industry concept, popular in places largely devoid of Jews, called "Jewish Heritage Sites." The term is a truly ingenious piece of marketing. "Jewish Heritage" is a phrase that sounds utterly benign, or to Jews, perhaps ever so slightly dutiful, suggesting a place that you surely ought to visit—after all, you came all this way, so how could you not? It is a much better name than "Property Seized from Dead or Expelled Jews." By calling these places "Jewish Heritage Sites," all those pesky moral concerns—about, say, why these "sites" exist to begin with—evaporate in a mist of goodwill. And not just goodwill, but goodwill aimed directly at you, the Jewish tourist. These non-Jewish citizens and their benevolent government have chosen to maintain this cemetery or renovate this synagogue or create this museum purely out of their profound respect for the Jews who once lived here (and who, for unstated reasons, no longer do)—and out of their sincere hope that you, the Jewish tourist, might someday arrive. But still, you cannot help but feel uncomfortable, and finally helpless, as you engage in the exact inverse of what Benjamin of Tudela once did: instead of traveling the world and visiting Jews, you are visiting their graves.

Harbin was enjoying a heat wave when I arrived, a balmy ten below with a wind chill of minus eighteen. I only needed to wear a pair of thermals, a shirt, a sweater, a fleece, a parka, a balaclava, a neck warmer, a hat, gloves, three pairs of socks, and three pairs of pants to go outdoors.

My first stop was the city's Jewish cemetery, billed by tour companies as the largest Jewish cemetery in the Far East— except that it's not a cemetery, since cemeteries contain dead bodies, and this one doesn't have any. In 1958, Harbin's local government was redesigning the city and decided that the Jewish cemetery, home to around 3,200 dead Jews, had to go. The city offered families the option of moving their dead relatives' graves to the site of a large Chinese cemetery called Huangshan, an hour's drive outside the city, for the price of about $50 per grave. Many Jewish families were long gone by then, so only 812 graves were moved—and, as it turned out, only the gravestones, since city authorities saw no reason to move the bodies too. The human remains from the old cemetery are now in what the Chinese call "deep burial"—that is, the space containing them has been paved over and turned into an amusement park. "It is nice for them to be there," my tour guide—whom I'll call Derek to keep him out of trouble—said of the dead Jews under the rides. "They are always with happy people now."

The drive to Huangshan took about an hour through industrial wastelands and frozen fields, culminating in a grandiose toll plaza with enormous Russian-style onion domes and then several miles more of abandoned warehouses, with a few bundled people by the roadside selling stacks of fake money to burn as offerings—because Huangshan is really a vast Chinese cemetery, filled with endless rows of identical shiny white tombstones on mini plots containing cremated remains. After driving past tens of thousands of dead Chinese people, we found the entrance to the cemetery's Jewish section, paid our fee, and entered the gates.

The Jewish section was compact and stately, with roughly seven hundred gravestones elaborately carved in Hebrew and Russian, along with many modern metal plaques sponsored by former Harbin Jews whose relatives' original stones hadn't been moved. Many of the original grave markers had ceramic inserts with photographic portraits of the deceased, which would have been intriguing if every single one hadn't been shattered or removed. The damage was clearly deliberate, which might explain why a cemetery employee kept following us around. The idea that Jewish cemetery desecration was currently in vogue in Harbin was a tad depressing, but to my surprise, this snowy Jewish Heritage Site didn't feel at all lonely or bereft. In fact, it was rather glam.

Inside the gate was a plaza with a massive granite Star of David sculpture, next to a two-story-high domed synagogue building festooned with more Stars of David. The synagogue's doors were locked, but through its windows I could see that the building was a shell, with nothing inside but some scattered tools and junk. When I asked what the building was for, Derek laughed. "They built it for Olmert's visit," he explained. "Now it's just used by the cemetery workers to stay warm." Ehud Olmert, a former Israeli prime minister who served prison time for corruption, had roots in Harbin. His father was born there, and his grandfather, or at least his grandfather's gravestone, was in Huangshan—a gravestone that had now been outdone by a twelve-foot-high black marble obelisk. The obelisk, crowned with yet another Jewish star, was carved with greetings written in English in Olmert's handwriting and painted in gold: "Thank you for protecting the memory of our family, and restoring dignity into [sic] the memory of those who were part of this community and [illegible] a reminder of a great Jewish life which a long time ago was part of Harbin." The words were a dashed-off scribble, suggesting that Olmert didn't quite expect them to be set in stone. His grandfather's gravestone had been replaced with a black-and-gold marble one to match the obelisk, outshining the plebeians with their smashed ceramic photos. Near his grave stood a trash can designed to look like a soccer ball.

Olmert's visit to Harbin in 2004 as Israel's deputy prime minister had been a big deal, but the (fake) synagogue built in his honor at the (also fake) cemetery was just one part of an enormous and expensive project on the part of the local provincial government to restore Jewish Heritage Sites. The government's explicit goal is to attract Jewish money, in the form of both tourism and investment by foreign Jews.

In our conversation, the One Jew of Harbin had only praise for these efforts, in which he has been deeply involved. "The restoration cost $30 million—it's unheard-of here. Everything was of the highest quality," Ben-Canaan told me, adding that Harbin's Jewish Heritage Sites have the same official designation as Chinese landmarks like the Forbidden City. But one of the many sources on Harbin he shared with me was a long 2007 news article from a Chinese magazine by a journalist named Su Ling, whom he described as one of China's rare investigative reporters. The article, titled "Harbin Jews: The Truth," traced a very particular history: not Harbin's Jewish Heritage, but the Heilongjiang provincial government's attempts to capitalize on that heritage.

The story began innocently enough, with a social-scientist-cum-real-estate-agent named Zhang Tiejiang, who discovered the prior Jewish ownership of many historic homes that he was supposed to demolish for a city planning project in 1992. Taking an interest, he studied the Jewish graves in Huangshan cemetery, translating their Russian text with the help of a computer program. His timing was auspicious: 1992 was the year China established diplomatic relations with Israel, and in 1999 China's premier made his first official visit to Jerusalem. Also auspicious: Heilongjiang Province, long reliant on declining industries like coal mining, had hit an economic slump. In

1999 Zhang Tiejiang published his idea in an article for a state news agency titled "Suggestions for the Study of Harbin Jews to Quicken Heilongjiang Economic Development."

This article made its way to the higher-ups in the Chinese government in Beijing, who dispatched an official to Heilongjiang's Academy of Social Sciences to "intensify the study of the history of Harbin Jews." A Center for Jewish Studies was established, with a massive budget enabling unqualified people producing minimal research to enjoy trips abroad. "Develop[ing] the travel industry and attracting business investments," the center's original website announced, was "the tenet of our existence and purpose." In years following, the government's $30 million produced far more tangible results, including not only the cemetery refurbishment but also the transformation of the New Synagogue into a Jewish museum, the reconstruction of the Old Synagogue and the Jewish secondary school, and the labeling of formerly Jewish-owned buildings as landmarks in the city's historic heart.

This attempt to "attract business investments" by researching Jewish history seems, to put it gently, statistically unsound. Among the tens of millions of tourists to China each year, forty thousand annual Israeli visitors and even fewer Jewish tourists from elsewhere amount to a rounding error. And the idea that Israeli or other Jewish-owned companies would be moved to invest in Heilongjiang Province out of nostalgia for its Jewish heritage seems unlikely at best. The only way to understand this thinking is to appreciate the role Jews play in the Chinese imagination.

Most Chinese people know next to nothing about Jews or

Judaism. But in a 2009 essay reviewing trends in Jewish studies in China, Lihong Song, a professor of Jewish studies at Nanjing University, pointed out a common pattern in what they do know. "My students' first association with Jews is that they are 'rich and smart,'" he noted. "The shelves of Chinese bookstores," Song explained, "are lined with bestsellers on Jewish subjects." What Jewish subjects might those be? Well, some of those bestselling titles are *Unveiling the Secrets of Jewish Success in the World Economy*, *What's Behind Jewish Excellence?*, *The Financial Empire of the Rothschilds*, *Talmudic Wisdom in Conducting Business*, and of course, *Talmud: The Greatest Jewish Bible for Making Money*. Song claimed that this was not antisemitic, but rather "some sort of Judeophilia."

At a 2007 "International Forum on Economic Cooperation between Harbin and the World's Jews," held in Harbin with dozens of invited Jewish guests who ranged from the Israeli ambassador to a group of Hungarian Jewish dentists, Harbin's mayor welcomed participants by citing esteemed Jews such as J. P. Morgan and John D. Rockefeller (neither of whom was Jewish). He then announced that "the world's money is in the pockets of the Americans, and the Americans' money is in the pockets of the Jews. This is the highest acclaim and praise to Jewish wisdom."

———————

Former Harbin Jews often remembered Harbin as a kind of paradise. "They owned the town," Irene Clurman, a daughter of former Harbin Jews, told me, describing the nostalgia that many "Harbintsy"—ex-Harbiners—expressed for their beloved city. "It was a semicolonial situation; they had Chinese servants and great schools and fur coats." Or in the words of her grandmother Roza (later Ethel) Clurman in a 1986 interview, "Harbin was a dream."

Roza Clurman's husband—Irene Clurman's grandfather—was kidnapped, tortured, and murdered in Harbin during the Japanese antisemitic reign of terror, after which his lucrative business (he introduced indoor plumbing to Manchuria) and his high-end rental building were confiscated, leaving his family with nothing. And the Clurman family's horror stories had begun much earlier: Roza Clurman was five during the 1905 Odessa pogrom, hiding in an attic for days on end while the neighborhood was ransacked and her neighbors murdered. The move to Harbin didn't quite prevent her family from being targeted, given that her husband also wound up murdered. But "my grandmother absolutely had a nostalgia for Harbin," Irene Clurman insisted. In her interview, Roza Clurman admitted that "everything changed" in Harbin, but she spent far more time describing its glory: the steaks the family ate, their household staff, the children's private lessons.

The ascent from pogroms to private lessons was dizzyingly fast, obscuring the community's equally precipitous decline. One Harbintsy descendant, Jean Ispa, told me how her father, an orphan, made his way to Harbin alone solely to study music, since Russian conservatories didn't take Jewish students. Running away from an orphanage, he collected scrap metal to buy a ticket to Harbin, where he was promptly jailed for entering the country illegally—and where musicians in the Jewish community bailed him out. "He was sixteen when he made this journey," Ispa told me in wonder. "He

gave concerts in Harbin. I even have the programs he played."
Another Harbin exile, Alexander Galatzky, was eight during
the pogroms of the 1919–1920 Russian Civil War, when he and
his mother repeatedly barricaded themselves in their apartment in Ukraine and listened to the screams of their neighbors being murdered and raped. When the ship fare his father
sent from New York was stolen, their only hope was to go east
to Manchuria, where his father planned to meet them. In rem-
iniscences he wrote down for his family, Galatzky described
boarding a cattle car to leave Ukraine: "Mother has a bundle
of old clothes with her. The soldier on guard of the cattle car
is trying to take it from her. She clutches at it, crying, kissing
the soldier's hand. We have no money or valuables and the old
clothes can be bartered for food en route. Without them we
would starve." After a life like that, Manchuria was paradise.

Of course, one could tell the same story about Russian
Jews who emigrated to New York. But in Harbin, where Russian Jews created their own Russian-Jewish bubble, their sense
of ownership and pride was greater—and that pride made the
story of their community's destruction into a footnote. Of the
Harbintsy descendants I interviewed, most mentioned friends
or relatives who were kidnapped, tortured, or murdered during the Japanese occupation. All had their family's hard-earned
assets seized by Manchuria's various regimes. But in the next
sentence they would tell me, again, how Harbin was "a golden
age." An entire organization in Israel, Igud Yotzei Sin (Association of Chinese Exiles), exists solely to connect homesick
"Chinese Jews" around the world with one another through
networking, social events, scholarships, and trilingual news-

letters which run to hundreds of pages. Until recent years, members gathered weekly in Tel Aviv to play mah-jongg, drink tea, and reminisce about the wonders of Harbin. Teddy Kaufman, who ran the organization until his death in 2012, published a memoir entitled *The Jews of Harbin Live On in My Heart*, extolling the Jewish paradise. His father was the community president who'd wound up in a gulag.

Harbin's Jewish "golden age" lasted less than one generation. Even before the Japanese occupation, things were unpleasant enough that leaving was, for many, a foregone conclusion. Alexander Galatzky, the boy whose mother bartered old clothes to feed him on the Trans-Siberian Railroad, kept diaries as a teenager from 1925 to 1929 that his daughter Bonnie Galat recently had translated. The diaries revealed an assumption that most teenagers don't live with: everyone planned to leave, and the only question was where to go. He counted off his friends' departures—to Palestine, to Russia, to Australia, to America—and waxed nostalgic about leaving, as he capitalized in his diary, "FOR GOOD." "My old classmate Misha leaves for Paris today," he wrote, describing one of many permanent goodbyes. "For good, I think . . . It's a scary word, 'FOR GOOD.' Biro left, and Pinsky, and I think I'm leaving next year too . . . and not with Mom and Dad, but alone." Galatzky's fears came true; the following year he left for Paris via train and ship through Shanghai, Ceylon, and Suez. Later he wound up supporting his parents, after they fled Harbin with little more than old clothes.

Many came to recall the community's destruction as if it were almost expected, like snow or rain. Alex Nahumson, who was born in Harbin and emigrated in 1950 at the age of three with his family, reports only "very happy memories" discussed by his parents. "The Chinese never did anything bad to us, just the Russians and the Japanese," he told me by phone in Hebrew from his home in Israel—despite the fact that his family's assets were plundered by the Maoist regime. "When my parents talked about Harbin, they only talked about their dacha [country home], the theater, the opera," he averred. When I brought up the kidnappings during the Japanese occupation, he verbally shrugged. "That's just crime," he insisted. "Crime happens everywhere." His parents survived all of these regime changes, he said cheerfully, "between the raindrops"—a Hebrew expression for evading repeated disaster. Losing everything they had was inevitable, like the weather. As the Russian Jewish writer Sholem Aleichem once put it, Jewish wealth is like snow in March, melting and washing away. Later in our conversation, Nahumson mentioned, almost casually, that his own grandfather was kidnapped and tortured by the Japanese.

———

It is hard to describe what, exactly, was wrong with Harbin's New Synagogue Jewish Museum—or as it said on my ticket, the "Construction Art Museum," a name that comes from the building's current ownership by the Harbin Municipal Construction Department. One feels the overwhelming need to applaud this (mostly) Jewish museum's mere existence, to carefully delineate its many strengths, to thank the locals for their bountiful goodwill. For it did have enormous strengths, and the goodwill was abundant. Still, from the moment I arrived at the large domed building and entered its wide-open space with an enormous Star of David decorating the floor—it only occurred to me later how ridiculous this detail was, since the floor would have been covered with seats when the synagogue was in use—I felt that creeping "Jewish Heritage" unease, the unarticulated sense that despite all the supposed goodwill, something was clearly off. But then my actual Jewish heritage kicked in, consisting of centuries of epigenetic instincts reminding me that I am only a guest. I swallowed my discomfort and started snapping pictures.

The Jewish history exhibition filled the second floor—the women's gallery of the synagogue. There, in vast arrays of photographs, I observed smiling, well-dressed people building synagogues, celebrating weddings, attending Zionist meetings, patronizing a library, posing in scout uniforms, working in a hospital, rescuing neighbors from a flood, and skating on the river. The displays were informative enough, even if their translated captions sometimes disintegrated into word salad. Beneath one portrait of a man wearing a prayer shawl and a tall clerical hat, for instance, the English caption read, "Judean assembly mark in harbin choir leading singer gram benefit maxwell minister radical." I asked Derek what the original Chinese caption meant. He smiled apologetically and said, "I'm not sure."

It was all admirably thorough, if a little garbled. But toward the far end of the gallery, on the part of the floor that had been constructed over the alcove where the ark for Torah scrolls once stood (the actual alcove for the ark is now a foyer leading to a restroom), I entered a set of little rooms whose contents puzzled me.

The first room was dominated by a large wooden desk, with a life-size white plaster sculpture of a bald and bearded Western man seated before an ancient paperless typewriter. The brass plaque in front of him read, "Real workplace of Jewish industrialist in Harbin." Confused by the word "real," I asked Derek if this was supposed to be a specific person. He glanced at the plaque and explained, "It is showing a Jew in Harbin. He is doing business."

In subsequent rooms, more tableaux of frozen Jews unfolded. There were life-size plaster Jews frozen at a grand piano, a life-size plaster Jew frozen in a chair with knitting needles, and two child-sized plaster Jews frozen on a bed, playing eternally with plaster blocks. This, the brass plaque informed me, was "The Display of the Jews' Family in Harbin." The plaque continued: "At the first half of the 20th century, not only was the display of the Jews' family simple, but also practical and the children lived a colorful life there." The children's blocks, like the children, were devoid of color. Later I discovered the unnamed inspiration for this display: Harbin's annual Snow Sculpture Park, full of figures carved from blocks of manufactured snow.

After the rooms full of frozen Jews, the photographs of mostly dead Jews resumed, dominated by "real Jewish industrialists" who "brought about numerous economic miracles" in Harbin, including the founders of Harbin's first sugar refinery, first soybean-export business, first candy factory, and China's first brewery. The wall text explained how Harbin "offered the Jews an opportunity for creating new enterprises and providing a solid foundation for their later economic activities in

Europe and America." This was true, I suppose, if one thinks of Harbin as a kind of business-school exercise, rather than a place where actual Jews created actual capital that was subsequently seized, transforming them overnight into penniless refugees, if they were lucky.

One enterprise prominently featured in the museum, for instance, was the Skidelsky Coal Mine Corporation. The Skidelskys were among the "Siberian Jews" who provided the initial capital for Harbin—although "initial capital" is an understatement. In an account of his family's holdings in *Prospect* magazine, Robert Skidelsky, a member of the British House of Lords and a Harbin native, described how his great-grandfather Leon Skidelsky held the contract in 1895—prior to Harbin's founding—to build the Trans-Siberian Railroad from Manchuria to Vladivostok. The Skidelskys were one of only ten Jewish families allowed to live in Vladivostok, since the railroad desperately needed them. They held long-term concessions on three thousand square kilometers of timber in Siberia and Manchuria, and enough long-term mining concessions to make them one of the region's largest employers. They continued supplying the railroad as it changed hands from the Russians to the Chinese to the Japanese. In 1924, Leon's son Solomon even charmed a local warlord into selling him a thirty-year lease on a mine, by repeatedly and deliberately losing to him in poker.

In 1945, Solomon Skidelsky was still nine years shy of running out the lease when the Soviets sent him and his brother to die in a gulag, and Communists—first Soviet and then Chinese—seized the mines. Decades later, Lord

Skidelsky filed his claim. "In 1984," Lord Skidelsky recounted, "I received a cheque for 24,000 English pounds in full settlement of a claim for compensation that amounted to £11 million." When he visited Harbin in 2006, local TV crews trailed him and presented him with flowers. The flowers were worth somewhat less than £11 million.

When I expressed my sense that the museum was telling only part of a story, Derek raised an issue that Ben-Canaan brought up with me repeatedly, that the museum focused exclusively on wealthy people—thus underscoring the idea that Jews are rich. "Obviously there were poor Jews here too," Derek pointed out. "The building across the street was the Jewish Free Kitchen."

It was only as I was leaving, through the enormous mezuzah-less door, that I looked back at what was once the sanctuary and understood what, exactly, was wrong. Above the vast Star of David floor, the museum was dominated by an enormous blown-up photograph of a 1930s farewell banquet, its rows of Harbin Jews in their tuxedos gathered to say goodbye to yet another Jewish family fleeing, as Alexander Galatzky had put it, "FOR GOOD." Suddenly the Jewish Heritage miasma melted away, and the realization hit me: Nothing in this museum explained why this glorious community no longer exists.

———

Harbin is a rather hideous city, its Soviet-style apartment blocks stretching as far as the eye can see. But the city's historic heart has been restored so thoroughly that if not for the

Chinese crowds and street signs, one could imagine being in prewar Europe. The restoration included turning the historic tree-lined Central Avenue into a pedestrian mall that doubles as an outdoor architectural museum, where each original building—80 percent of which were once Jewish-owned—is labeled with a plaque describing its past. Unfortunately the restoration also included installing loudspeakers that constantly blast high-volume Western music. When I arrived, they were playing "Edelweiss": *Bless my homeland forever.* The music made it hard to think.

Derek pointed out the various restored buildings on Central Avenue and elsewhere in the neighborhood: the Jewish-owned pharmacy, the Jewish Free Kitchen, the Jewish People's Bank, and many private homes, all now occupied by other enterprises. The "Heritage Architecture" plaques affixed to each historic building couldn't have been more direct: "This mansion," a typical one read, "was built by a Jew."

The most impressive Central Avenue building "built by a Jew" was the Modern Hotel, a building whose story captures the Harbin Jewish community's roller coaster of triumph and horror. The Modern Hotel was built by the Jewish entrepreneur Joseph Kaspe, and from the moment it opened in 1909, it was the height of Manchurian chic. The Modern wasn't merely a high-class establishment frequented by celebrities and diplomats. Its premises also included China's first movie theater, and the hotel frequently hosted theatrical performances, lectures, and concerts with seating for hundreds. Kaspe also created other Modern-labeled luxury products like jewelry and high-end food. In other words, the Modern was a brand.

When the Japanese occupied Harbin, they immediately set their sights on the Modern. But Joseph Kaspe was one step ahead of them. His wife and two sons had moved to Paris, where they had acquired French citizenship—so Kaspe put the Modern in his son's name and raised the French flag over the hotel. He assumed the Japanese wouldn't risk an international incident just to steal his business. He was wrong.

In 1932, Kaspe invited his older son Semion, a celebrated pianist, back to Manchuria for a concert tour. On the last night of his tour, Semion was kidnapped. Instead of paying the bankruptcy-inducing ransom, Joseph Kaspe went to the French consulate. It didn't help; the kidnappers upped the ante, mailing Kaspe his son's ear. After three months, Semion's body was found outside the city. When Kaspe saw his son's maimed and gangrenous corpse, he went insane. Friends shipped him off to Paris, where he died in 1938. His wife was deported and died at Auschwitz five years later. His younger son escaped to Mexico, where he died in 1996, refusing to ever discuss Harbin.

The Modern Hotel is still in operation today, though at a few stars lower than the Holiday Inn where I stayed down the street. The large pink stone building with its glamorous arched windows and turrets still dominates Central Avenue, its girth expanding for an entire city block, Cyrillic letters spelling out "MODERN" running down one corner of its facade. Outside, I saw a long line of people winding its way down the street toward one end of the hotel, the hordes queuing in minusten degrees. The line, Derek explained, was for the Modern's famous ice cream. "In Harbin, we love eating cold foods at cold temperatures," he said with a grin. It's true; the streets of Harbin are lined with snack stands selling skewers of frozen fruit. The Kaspes figured this out and created China's first commercially produced ice cream, sold today under the chic English-language brand name "Modern 1906." (The three-year error on the brand's founding date clearly troubled no one but me.) Passing up the frozen treats, I went inside.

The Modern Hotel's lobby was shabby and nondescript, except for an exhibit celebrating the hotel's illustrious history. It began with a bronze bust of Joseph Kaspe, with wall text in Chinese and English describing the accomplishments of the Modern Corporation and its founder, "The Jew of Russian Nationality Mr. Alexander Petrovich Kaspe." (The "Alexander" was inexplicable; Joseph Kaspe's actual first name appeared in Russian on the bust.) As the wall text explained, this impressive Jew founded a "flagship business in Harbin integrated with hotel, cinema, jewelry store, etc." "In recent years," the text continued, "the cultural brand of Modern is continuously consolidated and developed." It then listed the numerous businesses held by this storied company— including the Harbin Ice Festival, which belonged to the Modern Corporation until the provincial government took it over a few years ago. "Currently," the wall text gloated, "Modern Group . . . is riding on momentum, and is shaping a brand-new international culture industry innovation platform." Mr. Kaspe's descendants would indeed be proud of this heritage, if any of them had inherited it.

But after all, the Modern Hotel clearly honors its Jewish Heritage! There, on its walls, were enlarged photos of

Joseph Kaspe's family, including his murdered son, sexy in his white tie and tails, frozen over his piano. There, under glass, were Real Historic Items from the Kaspe family, including silver candlesticks, an old-timey telephone, and a samovar! And there, in one particularly dusty glass case near the floor, were "the Kaspe collection of household utensils of Judaism sacrificial offerings," including an actual Passover Seder plate!

I squatted down for a closer look at this display and saw that there were two plates inside it. The Seder plate had a bronzy Judaica motif suspiciously familiar from my own American Jewish childhood. I squelched my skepticism until I saw that it was carved all around with English words. The second plate, a ceramic one, sported an Aztec-esque design, with the word "Mexico" painted across the bottom—a 1980s airport souvenir. At that point it became clear that any Real Historic Items from the Kaspes had long disappeared into some regime's pockets, and that this display had been sourced from eBay.

I put my balaclava back on and went out into the cold again, past the hundreds of Chinese people clamoring for Kaspe's ice cream, and headed to the Old Synagogue, which is now a concert hall. The result of a multimillion-dollar renovation project for which the One Jew of Harbin served as an adviser, the building is part of an entire "Jewish block" that includes the music school next door, which was once the Jewish secondary school. Ben-Canaan was meticulous about the project, gathering and examining old photographs and descriptions to exactly replicate the ark with its granite Ten Commandments motif, the pillars, the gallery that was once the women's section, and the seats with their prayer-book stands. His only concession, he told me, was to make the bimah (the platform before the ark) wide enough to accommodate a chamber orchestra. When the person manning the ticket booth refused to let me peek inside, I bought a ticket for that night's string quartet.

The Old Synagogue's interior shocked me. I don't know what I was expecting, but what I didn't expect was to be standing in a synagogue no different from every single urban early-twentieth-century synagogue I've ever entered around the world, from my own former synagogue in New York City to others as far as London and Moscow and Cape Town and Buenos Aires and Melbourne—all those buildings around the world where you walk into the sanctuary (usually after passing an armed guard) and could literally be in any synagogue anywhere, which is exactly the point. The One Jew of Harbin did a marvelous job—so marvelous that as I walked into the large hall and saw the massive ark looming before me, with its familiar Hebrew inscription imploring me to *Know Before Whom You Stand*, I instinctively listened for what part of the service I was walking in on, how late I was this time, whether they were up to the Torah reading yet. My thoughts about how far back I should sit finally gave way to logic, and I looked at the seat number on my ticket.

But when I took my seat in the third row, I still could not shut down my muscle memory. My hands went straight to the slot in the seat in front of me, reaching for a prayer book that wasn't there. I almost couldn't stop myself from reciting all the words I've recited in rooms like this, the words I've repeated my entire life, the same words recited by all the people who have gathered in rooms like this over the past twenty centuries, in Yavneh and Pumbedita and Aleppo and Rome and Marrakesh and Philadelphia and Mumbai and São Paulo and Harbin, facing Jerusalem. I was awed, googly-eyed. In that moment I suddenly knew, in a vast sense that expanded far beyond space and time, before whom I stand.

Then a Chinese string quartet walked up to the bimah in front of the ark, and instead of bowing before the ark, they bowed before me. The lights dropped, and they played, spectacularly well, Brahms's "Hungarian Dance Number 5," and Tchaikovsky's "Romeo and Juliet," and inexplicably, "Cotton-Eyed Joe."

And suddenly I was very, very tired.

———

Somewhere in between the synagogues, the Belle Epoque–style bookstore named for Nikolai Gogol, the pool carved out of the frozen river with people swimming in minus-thirty degrees, and the hundreds of dead Jews, I found myself in a "Siberian Tiger Park," where seven hundred of the world's remaining tigers loll behind high chain-link fences or pace in isolation cells, in what resembles a tiger reeducation camp. There, after riding a bus painted with tiger stripes through bare icy yards full of catatonic-looking tigers, I was encouraged to buy slabs of raw meat—since, as Derek explained, the facility only provided the animals with meager rations, with the assumption that tourists would make up the difference. The pull of curiosity tainted by guilt—a feeling remarkably similar to my "Jewish Heritage" unease—brought me to a woman selling buckets of raw pork slabs, which visitors feed to the tigers with tongs through the chain link. The woman selling the slabs also offered a crate of live chickens that I could alternatively have purchased as tiger food; this would have involved buying a live chicken and thrusting it into the tiger enclosure via a dedicated chicken chute. For the first time in my life, I bought pork.

As I struggled to pick up slippery pieces of meat with the tongs, I remembered a moment in the Talmud (*The Greatest Jewish Bible for Making Money*) when the rabbis claim that the last thing created during the week of creation was the world's first pair of tongs, since tongs can only be forged with other tongs—a story whose haunting image of human limits transcends its lack of logic. When I succeeded in wielding the meat, the otherwise catatonic tigers pounced against the fence at me in a cartoon-like fury, rattling the Soviet-style barriers as they battled one another for the strips of flesh. I watched these almost mythic captives through a thick haze of pity and fear, helplessly flinging inadequate scraps at something powerful, beautiful, and trapped. Much later, I came across a *National Geographic* article claiming that this "park" was in fact a tiger farm, where these endangered animals— only seven of which still exist in the northeastern Chinese

wild, thus outnumbering Jews in the region by 700 percent—
were bred and slaughtered for trophies and traditional medicines.
It all felt like an elaborate con. Or if not quite a con, a *display*.

The Harbin Ice Festival was the greatest display of all, sur-
passing my most fevered expectations. It was much, much
larger and more elaborate than I had imagined from the photos and videos that had lured me to Harbin. I'd been amply
warned by online strangers about how difficult the festival
would be to endure, since it requires long periods outside,
at night, in punishing temperatures. But once I was there, I
was shocked by how easy it was. All I needed to add to my
Harbin ensemble was a second sweater, a fourth pair of pants,
a second pair of gloves, a fourth pair of socks, handwarmers
stuck into my gloves and boots, and ice cleats, and I was good
to go. I had been told that I wouldn't be able to bear the cold
for more than forty minutes. In the company of approximately
ten thousand others who were also visiting that evening, a
number relatively insignificant in the vastness of the festival, I
stayed for three hours.

Among the ice castles and ice fortresses clustered around
a snow Buddha the size of a high school, I recognized shim-
mering tacky neon versions of places I'd visited in real life,
cataloging them in my brain like Benjamin of Tudela: the Wild
Goose Pagoda of Xian, the Summer Palace outside Beijing,
the gate to the Forbidden City, Chartres Cathedral, the Cam-
panile tower near Venice's original Jewish ghetto, the Colos-
seum built by Jewish slaves brought from Jerusalem to Rome. I
wandered around and through these flashing structures, their

colors changing every few seconds as the LED wiring blinked within each ice block, passing over bridges and through moon gates and up staircases and down slides that wound their way through castles of ice. China is a place full of enormous, gaudy, extravagantly impersonal monuments made possible through cheap labor, from a two-thousand-year-old tomb filled with ten thousand terra cotta warriors in Xian to the medieval Great Wall outside Beijing to the 1994 Oriental Pearl Tower in Shanghai. The Harbin Ice Festival was the gargantuan fluorescent opposite of intimate or subtle. It was mind-blowing, and mindless. It was the most astounding man-made thing I had ever seen.

What was most shocking about the Ice Festival was the bizarre fact that all of it was temporary. In another month or two, the vast city would begin to melt. But unlike what I ignorantly assumed, the ice city does not simply vanish on its own. Instead, when the melting begins, ten thousand workers return to hack apart the millions of ice blocks, remove their electrical wiring, and then haul them out and dump them in the river. Like all cities, there is nothing natural about its creation, and also nothing natural about its destruction.

Nothing simply disappears. As I left Harbin, I thought of Hannah Agre, the Last Jew of Harbin—the crazy old lady who refused to leave the city, who died alone in 1985, twenty-three years after the last Jewish family left, in an office space that she had rejiggered into an apartment on the second floor of the Old Synagogue. It occurred to me, as I passed through the industrial wastelands and endless high-rises on my way to the Harbin airport, that maybe she wasn't so crazy. Maybe she didn't like being told to leave. Maybe she was physically enacting what all the other Harbintsy spent the rest of their lives trying to do, as they gathered in San Francisco and Tel Aviv to play mah-jongg and share photos of their samovars and fur coats. Maybe she wanted to keep the castle her family had built, preserved in ice.

By the time I reached the airport, the Harbin Holiday Inn's breakfast buffet of dragon fruit and lychee nuts was a distant memory, and I was hungry. Fortunately, right next to my gate there was a hip-looking eatery, with historic black-and-white photos framed on trendy brick walls. Its sign read: "Modern 1906."

I almost couldn't believe it, but yes, here it was once more: Joseph Kaspe's business. As if responding to my private disbelief, a giant flat screen on a hip brick wall flashed a photo of Kaspe's family, then one of Kaspe's face. I stared at the photos before they blinked away, looking at this murdered family and then at Kaspe, the man who built a city only to lose his son, his property, and his mind. I suddenly felt shaken by the "success" of this business that has apparently persisted uninterrupted for over a century, by the sheer chutzpah of this open bragging about a corporate "heritage," by the enduring quality of stolen goods. It was twenty below outside, but I bought an ice cream in a flavor labeled "Original." The sweet frozen cream melted in my mouth, gone before I even put away my Chinese change.

I was in the last row of the Air China plane leaving Harbin, the only Westerner on board. There was an intense smell of barbecued pork as someone in the row in front of me celebrated the Year of the Pig. I thought of Alexander Galatzky leaving Harbin "FOR GOOD," boarding the train to Shanghai and then the boat to Ceylon and on through the Suez Canal, a journey embarked upon nine years after he first traversed the world at the age of nine on the Trans-Siberian Railroad, with his mother and her bag of old clothes. A cheerful animated panda on the screen in front of me explained the many safety features of the aircraft, including what to do if we should require, as the awkward English translation put it, "Emergency Ditching." I thought of the Clurmans, the Kaspes, the Nahumsons moving between the raindrops, ditching as needed, ditching as expected, ditching a foregone conclusion. I watched the animation and remembered Benjamin of Tudela, the chipper cartoon of the perilous journey around the world, where every Jewish community was documented and counted and marveled at, full of cheery animated people who never felt the need to ditch, where cities never melted away.

Within two minutes of takeoff, Harbin was no longer visible. Outside my window, I saw only snow-dusted farmland and the gleam of sunlight on the frozen river. The land was vast and empty. The enormous city was gone.

Chapter 3

DEAD
AMERICAN JEWS,
PART ONE

"THERE ARE NO WORDS."

This was what I heard most frequently from good people stunned by the news one Saturday morning in October of 2018: eleven people murdered at a Pittsburgh synagogue, the largest massacre of Jews in American history. But there are words for this, entire books full of words: the books the murdered people were reading at the hour of their deaths. News reports described these victims as praying, but Jewish prayer is not primarily personal or spontaneous. It is communal reading: public recitations of ancient words, scripts compiled centuries ago and nearly identical in every synagogue in the world. A lot of those words are about exactly this.

When I told my children what had happened, they didn't

ask why; they knew. "Because some people hate Jews," they said. How did these American children know that? They shrugged. "It's like the Passover story," they told me. "And the Hanukkah story. And the Purim story. And the Babylonians. And the Romans." My children are descendants of Holocaust survivors, but they didn't need to go that far forward in history. The words were already there.

The people murdered in Pittsburgh were mostly old, because the old are the pillars of Jewish life, full of days and memories. They are the ones who come to synagogue first, the ones who know the words by heart. The oldest victim at the Tree of Life synagogue was Rose Mallinger, age ninety-seven.

The year Mallinger was born was the tail end of the mass migration of over a million Eastern European Jews to America. Many brought with them memories of pogroms, of men invading synagogues with weapons, of blood on holy books. This wasn't shocking, because it was already described in those books. On Yom Kippur in synagogue, these Jews read the stories of rabbis murdered by the Romans, including Rabbi Haninah ben Teradion, who was wrapped in a Torah scroll set aflame. Before dying, he told his students, "The parchment is burning, but the letters are flying free!" My synagogue's old High Holiday prayer book, a classic edition edited by Rabbi Morris Silverman that dominated twentieth-century American synagogues, hints at what these stories meant to American Jews of Ms. Mallinger's age. Its 1939 English preface asks: "Who can forget, even after decades, the sight of his father huddled in the great prayer shawl and trying in vain to conceal the tears which flowed down his cheeks during the recital of this poem?" By the time I was a kid reciting those poetic stories, no one was crying. Instead, my siblings and I smirked at the excessive gory details, the violence unfamiliar enough to be absurd. But Rabbi Haninah must have been right, because we were still reading from that same scroll, the same words Jews first taught the world: *Do not oppress the stranger. Love your neighbor as yourself.*

People Ms. Mallinger's age were in their twenties when word spread about mass murders of Jews in Europe. In synagogue on Rosh Hashanah, they read the old words begging God for compassion, "for the sake of those killed for your holy name," and "for the sake of those slaughtered for your uniqueness." My husband's grandparents came here after those massacres, their previous spouses and children slaughtered like the people in the prayer. They kept reciting the prayer, and for their new American family it reverted to metaphor.

In the decades that followed, Jews from other places joined American synagogues, many bringing memories that American Jews had forgotten. Those memories were waiting for them in the synagogue's books. On the holiday of Purim, they recited the Book of Esther, about an ancient Persian leader's failed attempt at a Jewish genocide. It's a time for costumes and levity, for shaking noisemakers to blot out the evildoer's name. One year my brother dressed as the ayatollah, and the Persians in our congregation laughed. Another year someone dressed as Gorbachev; the Russians loved it. The evildoers seemed defeated.

In 2000, when Ms. Mallinger was seventy-nine, a Jewish senator was his party's nominee for vice president. A year later the White House hosted its first official Hanukkah party. About a decade later I attended one myself. In the White House we recited ancient words thanking God for rescuing us from hatred. To older Jews, this felt miraculous: My parents and grandfather gawked at my photos, awestruck. But at the party I met younger Jewish leaders who often attended these events. To them, this was normal. The ancient hatred was a memory, words on a page.

Or maybe it wasn't. In 2001, after terrorists attacked American cities, concrete barriers sprouted in front of my family's synagogue, police cruisers parked in the lot. This felt practical in a nation on edge; we assumed it affected everyone. As my children were born and grew, the barriers and guards became their normal. When I took my children to an interfaith Thanksgiving service at a church down the street from our synagogue, one of them asked me why no one was guarding the door.

In the years that followed, the internet suddenly allowed anyone to say whatever they wanted, rewarding the most outrageous from every political stripe. Soon, comments sections became an open sewer, flowing with centuries-old garbage—and as social media exploded, those comments evolved into open vitriol, as abstract hate scaled up to direct verbal attacks on Jewish institutions and individuals. To young Jews this felt confusing. To old Jews it must have felt familiar, a memory passed down and echoed in the holy books.

When Ms. Mallinger was ninety-seven, she and ten other Jews were murdered in their synagogue. There are words for this too, a Hebrew phrase for 2,500 years' worth of people

murdered for being Jews: *kiddush hashem*, death in sanctification of God's name.

My children were right: This story is old, with far too
many words. Yet they were wrong about one thing. In the old
stories, those outside the community rarely helped or cared;
our ancestors' consolation came only from one another and
from God. But in this horrific new reality, perhaps our old
words might mean something new.

When they return to synagogue, mourners are greeted
with more ancient words: "May God comfort you among the
mourners of Zion and Jerusalem." In that verse, the word used
for God is *hamakom*—literally, "the place." *May the place comfort you.*

May the people in this place comfort you: the first respond-
ers who rush to your rescue, the neighbors who overwhelm
evil with kindness, the Americans of every background who
inspire more optimism than Jewish history allows. May this
country comfort you, with its infinite promise. As George
Washington vowed in his 1790 letter to a Rhode Island synagogue, America shall be a place where "every one shall sit in
safety under his own vine and fig tree, and there shall be none
to make him afraid." Those words aren't his. They're from the
Hebrew prophet Micah, on the shelves of every synagogue in
the world.

In synagogue as always, we read from the scroll we call
the Tree of Life, and the place will comfort us. As we put the
book away, we repeat the words from Lamentations: "Renew
our days as of old."

Chapter 4

EXECUTED

JEWS

ALA ZUSKIN PERELMAN AND I HAD BEEN IN TOUCH online before I finally met her in person, and I still cannot quite believe that she exists. Years ago, I wrote a novel about Marc Chagall and the Yiddish-language artists whom he once knew in Russia, all of whom were eventually murdered by the Soviet regime. While researching the novel, I found myself sucked into the bizarre story of these people's exploitation and destruction: how the Soviet Union first welcomed these artists as exemplars of universal human ideals, then used them for its own purposes, and finally executed them. I named my main character after the executed Yiddish actor Benjamin Zuskin, a comic performer known for playing fools. After the book came out, I heard from Ala in an email written in halting English: "I am Benjamin Zuskin's daughter." That winter I was speaking at a literary conference in Israel, where Ala lived, and she and I arranged to meet. It was like meeting a character from a book.

My hosts had generously put me up with other writers in a beautiful stone house in Jerusalem. We were there during Hanukkah, the celebration of Jewish independence. On the first night of the holiday, I walked to Jerusalem's Old City and watched as people lit enormous Hanukkah torches at the Western Wall. I thought of my home in New Jersey, where in school growing up I sang fake English Hanukkah songs created by American music education companies at school Christmas concerts, with lyrics describing Hanukkah as being about "joy and peace and love." Joy and peace and love describe Hanukkah, a commemoration of an underdog military victory over a powerful empire, about as well as they describe the Fourth of July. I remembered challenging a chorus teacher about one such song, and being told that I was a poor sport for disliking joy and peace and love. (Imagine a "Christmas song" with lyrics celebrating Christmas, the holiday of freedom. Doesn't everyone like freedom? What pedant would reject such a song?) I sang those words in front of hundreds of people to satisfy my neighbors that my tradition was universal—meaning, just like theirs. The night before meeting Ala, I walked back to the house through the dense stone streets of the Old City's Jewish Quarter, where every home had a glass case by its door, displaying the holiday's oil lamps. It was strange to see those hundreds of glowing lights. They were like a shining announcement that this night of celebration was shared by all these strangers around me, that it was universal. The experience was so unfamiliar that I didn't know what to make of it.

The next morning, Ala knocked on the door of the stone house and sat down in its living room, with its view of the Old City. She was a small dark-haired woman whose perfect posture showed a firmness that belied her age. She looked at me and said in Hebrew, "I feel as if you knew my father, like you understood what he went through. How did you know?"

The answer to that question goes back several thousand years.

––––––––––

The teenage boys who participated in competitive athletics in the gymnasium in Jerusalem 2,200 years ago had their circumcisions reversed, because otherwise they wouldn't have been allowed to play. In the Hellenistic empire that had conquered Judea, sports were sacred, the entry point to being a person who mattered, the ultimate height of cool—and sports, of course, were always played in the nude. As one can imagine, ancient genital surgery of this nature was excruciating and potentially fatal. But the boys did not want to miss out.

I learned this fun fact in seventh grade, from a Hebrew school teacher who was instructing me and my pubescent classmates about the Hanukkah story—about how Hellenistic tyranny gained a foothold in ancient Judea with the help of Jews who wanted to fit in. This teacher seemed overly jazzed to talk about penises with a bunch of adolescents, and I suspected he'd made the whole thing up. At home, I decided to fact-check. I pulled a dusty old book off my parents' shelf, Volume One of Heinrich Graetz's opus *History of the Jews*.

In nineteenth-century academic prose, Graetz explained how the leaders of Judea demonstrated their loyalty to the occupying Hellenistic empire by building a gymnasium and recruiting teenage athletes—only to discover that "in uncovering their bodies they could immediately be recognized as Judeans. But were they to take part in the Olympian games, and expose themselves to the mockery of Greek scoffers? Even this difficulty they evaded by undergoing a painful operation, so as to disguise the fact that they were Judeans." Their Zeus-worshiping overlords were not fooled. Within a few years, the regime outlawed not only circumcision but all of Jewish religious practice, and put to death anyone who didn't comply.

Sometime after that, the Maccabees showed up. That's the part of the story we usually hear.

Those ancient Jewish teenagers were on my mind that Hanukkah when Ala came to tell me about her father's terrifying life, because I sensed that something profound united them—something that doesn't match what we're usually taught about what bigotry looks or feels like. It doesn't involve "intolerance" or "persecution," at least not at first. Instead, it looks likes the Jews themselves are choosing to reject their own traditions. It is a form of weaponized shame.

Two distinct patterns of antisemitism can be identified by the Jewish holidays that celebrate triumphs over them: Purim and Hanukkah. In the Purim version of antisemitism, exemplified by the Persian genocidal decrees in the biblical Book of Esther, the goal is openly stated and unambiguous: Kill all the Jews. In the Hanukkah version of antisemitism, whose appearances range from the Spanish Inquisition to the Soviet regime, the goal is still to eliminate Jewish civilization. But in the Hanukkah version, this goal could theoretically be accomplished simply by destroying Jewish civilization, while leaving the warm, de-Jewed bodies of its former practitioners intact.

For this reason, the Hanukkah version of antisemitism often employs Jews as its agents. It requires not dead Jews but cool Jews: those willing to give up whatever specific aspect of Jewish civilization is currently uncool. Of course, Judaism has always been uncool, going back to its origins as the planet's only monotheism, featuring a bossy and unsexy invisible God. Uncoolness is pretty much Judaism's brand, which is why cool people find it so threatening—and why Jews who are willing to become cool are absolutely necessary to Hanukkah anti-semitism's success. These "converted" Jews are used to demonstrate the good intentions of the regime—which of course isn't antisemitic but merely requires that its Jews publicly flush thousands of years of Jewish civilization down the toilet in exchange for the worthy prize of not being treated like dirt, or not being murdered. For a few years. Maybe.

I wish I could tell the story of Ala's father concisely, compellingly, the way everyone prefers to hear about dead Jews. I regret to say that Benjamin Zuskin wasn't minding his own business and then randomly stuffed into a gas chamber, that his thirteen-year-old daughter did not sit in a closet writing an uplifting diary about the inherent goodness of humanity, that he did not leave behind sad-but-beautiful aphorisms pondering the absence of God while conveniently letting his fellow humans off the hook. He didn't even get crucified for his beliefs. Instead, he and his fellow Soviet Jewish artists—extraordinarily

intelligent, creative, talented, and empathetic adults—were
played for fools, falling into a slow-motion psychological horror story brimming with suspense and twisted self-blame. They
were lured into a long game of appeasing and accommodating,
giving up one inch after another of who they were in order to
win that grand prize of being allowed to live.

Spoiler alert: they lost.

I was in graduate school studying Yiddish literature, itself a
rich vein of discussion about such impossible choices, when I
became interested in Soviet Jewish artists like Ala's father. As
I dug through library collections of early-twentieth-century
Yiddish works, I came across a startling number of poetry
books illustrated by Marc Chagall. I wondered if Chagall had
known these Yiddish writers whose works he illustrated, and
it turned out that he had. One of Chagall's first jobs as a young
man was as an art teacher at a Jewish orphanage near Moscow, built for children orphaned by Russia's 1919–1920 civil war
pogroms. This orphanage had a rather renowned faculty, populated by famous Yiddish writers who trained these trauma-
tized children in the healing art of creativity.

It all sounded very lovely, until I noticed something else.
That Chagall's art did not rely on a Jewish language—that
it had, to use that insidious phrase, "universal appeal"—
allowed him a chance to succeed as an artist in the West.
The rest of the faculty, like Chagall, had also spent years in
western Europe before the Russian revolution, but they chose
to return to Russia because of the Soviet Union's policy of

endorsing Yiddish as a "national Soviet language." In the 1920s and '30s, the USSR offered unprecedented material support to Yiddish culture, paying for Yiddish-language schools, theaters, publishing houses, and more, to the extent that there were Yiddish literary critics who were salaried by the Soviet government. This support led the major Yiddish novelist Dovid Bergelson to publish his landmark 1926 essay "Three Centers," about New York, Warsaw, and Moscow as centers of Yiddish-speaking culture, asking which city offered Yiddish writers the brightest prospects. His unequivocal answer was Moscow, a choice that brought him back to Russia the following year, where many other Jewish artists joined him.

But Soviet support for Jewish culture was part of a larger plan to brainwash and coerce national minorities into submitting to the Soviet regime—and for Jews, it came at a very specific price. From the beginning, the regime eliminated anything in the celebrated Jewish "nationality" that didn't suit its needs. Jews were awesome, provided they weren't practicing the Jewish religion, studying traditional Jewish texts, using Hebrew, or supporting Zionism. The Soviet Union thus pioneered a versatile gaslighting slogan, which it later spread through its client states in the developing world and which remains popular today: it was not antisemitic, merely anti-Zionist. (In the process of not being antisemitic and merely being anti-Zionist, the regime managed to persecute, imprison, torture, and murder thousands of Jews.) What's left of Jewish culture once you surgically remove religious practice, traditional texts, Hebrew, and Zionism? In the Soviet Empire, one answer was Yiddish, but Yiddish was also suspect for its supposedly backward elements. Nearly 15 percent of its words came directly from biblical and rabbinic Hebrew, so Soviet Yiddish schools and publishers, under the guise of "simplifying" spelling, implemented a new and quite literally antisemitic spelling system that eliminated those words' ancient Near Eastern roots. Another answer was "folklore"—music, visual art, theater, and other creative work reflecting Jewish life—but of course most of that cultural material was also deeply rooted in biblical and rabbinic sources, or reflected common religious practices like Jewish holidays and customs, so that was treacherous too.

No, what the regime required were Yiddish stories that showed how horrible traditional Jewish practice was, stories in which happy, enlightened Yiddish-speaking heroes rejected both religion and Zionism (which, aside from its modern political form, is also a fundamental feature of ancient Jewish texts and prayers traditionally recited at least three times daily). This de-Jewing process is clear from the repertoire of the government-sponsored Moscow State Yiddish Theater, which could only present or adapt Yiddish plays that denounced traditional Judaism as backward, bourgeois, corrupt, or even more explicitly—as in the many productions involving ghosts and graveyard scenes—as dead. As its actors would be, soon enough.

The Soviet Union's destruction of Jewish culture commenced, in a calculated move, with Jews positioned as the destroyers. It began with the Yevsektsiya, committees of Jewish Bolsheviks whose paid government jobs from 1918 through 1930 were to persecute, imprison, and occasionally murder

Jews who participated in religious or Zionist institutions—
categories that included everything from synagogues to sports
clubs, all of which were shut down and their leaders either
exiled or "purged." This went on, of course, until the regime
purged the Yevsektsiya members themselves.

The pattern repeated in the 1940s. As sordid as the
Yevsektsiya chapter was, I found myself more intrigued by
the undoing of the Jewish Antifascist Committee, a board of
prominent Soviet Jewish artists and intellectuals established
by Joseph Stalin in 1942 to drum up financial support from
Jews overseas for the Soviet war effort. Two of the more
prominent names on the JAC's roster of talent were Solomon
Mikhoels, the director of the Moscow State Yiddish Theater,
and Ala's father Benjamin Zuskin, the theater's leading actor.
After promoting these people during the war, Stalin decided
these loyal Soviet Jews were no longer useful, and charged
them all with treason. He had decided that this committee he
himself had created was in fact a secret Zionist cabal, designed
to bring down the Soviet state. Mikhoels was murdered first,
in a 1948 hit staged to look like a traffic accident. Nearly all the
others—Zuskin and twelve more Jewish luminaries, including the novelist Dovid Bergelson, who had proclaimed Moscow as the center of the Yiddish future—were executed by
firing squad on August 12, 1952.

Just as the regime accused these Jewish artists and intellectuals of being too "nationalist" (read: Jewish), today's long
hindsight makes it strangely tempting to read this history and
accuse them of not being "nationalist" enough—that is, of
being so foolishly committed to the Soviet regime that they

were unable to see the writing on the wall. Many works on this subject have said as much. In *Stalin's Secret Pogrom*, the indispensable English translation of transcripts from the JAC "trial," Russia scholar Joshua Rubenstein concludes his lengthy introduction with the following:

> As for the defendants at the trial, it is not clear what they believed about the system they each served. Their lives darkly embodied the tragedy of Soviet Jewry. A combination of revolutionary commitment and naïve idealism had tied them to a system they could not renounce. Whatever doubts or misgivings they had, they kept to themselves, and served the Kremlin with the required enthusiasm. They were not dissidents. They were Jewish martyrs. They were also Soviet patriots. Stalin repaid their loyalty by destroying them.

This is completely true, and also completely unfair. The tragedy—even the term seems unjust, with its implied blaming of the victim—was not that these Soviet Jews sold their souls to the devil, though many clearly did. The tragedy was that integrity was never an option in the first place.

———————

Ala was almost thirteen years old when her father was arrested, and until that moment she was immersed in the Soviet Yiddish artistic scene. Her mother was also an actor in the Moscow State Yiddish Theater; her family lived in the same building as the murdered theater director Solomon Mikhoels, and moved in the same circles as other Jewish actors and writers. After seeing her parents perform countless times, Ala had a front-row seat to the destruction of their world. She attended Mikhoels's state funeral, heard about the arrest of the brilliant Yiddish author Der Nister from an actor friend who witnessed it from her apartment across the hall, and was present when secret police ransacked her home in conjunction with her father's arrest. In her biography of her father, *The Travels of Benjamin Zuskin*, she provides for her readers what she gave me that morning in Jerusalem: an emotional recounting, with the benefit of hindsight, of what it was really like to live through the Soviet Jewish nightmare.

It's as close as we can get, anyway. Her father Benjamin Zuskin's own thoughts on the topic are available only from state interrogations extracted under unknown tortures. (One typical interrogation document from his three and a half years in the notorious Lubyanka Prison announces that that day's interrogation lasted four hours, but the transcript is only half a page long—leaving to the imagination how interrogator and interrogatee may have spent their time together. Suffice it to say that another JAC detainee didn't make it to the trial alive.) His years in prison began when he was arrested in December of 1948 in a Moscow hospital room, where he was being treated for chronic insomnia brought on by the murder of his boss and career-long acting partner, Mikhoels; the secret police strapped him to a gurney and carted him to prison in his hospital gown while he was still sedated.

But in order to truly appreciate the loss here, one needs to know what was lost—to return to the world of the great

Yiddish writer Sholem Aleichem, the author of Benjamin Zuskin's first role on the Yiddish stage, in a play fittingly titled *It's a Lie!*

Benjamin Zuskin's path to the Yiddish theater and later to the Soviet firing squad began in a shtetl comparable to those immortalized in Sholem Aleichem's work. Zuskin, a child from a traditional family who was exposed to theater only through traveling Yiddish troupes and clowning relatives, experienced that world's destruction: his native Lithuanian shtetl, Ponievezh, was among the many Jewish towns forcibly evacuated during the First World War, catapulting him and hundreds of thousands of other Jewish refugees into modernity. He landed in Penza, a city with professional Russian theater and Yiddish amateur troupes. In 1920, the Moscow State Yiddish Theater opened, and by 1921, Zuskin was starring alongside Mikhoels, the theater's leading light.

In the one acting class I have ever attended, I learned only one thing: acting isn't about pretending to be someone you aren't, but rather about emotional communication. Zuskin, who not only starred in most productions but also taught in the theater's acting school, embodied that concept. His very first audition was a one-man sketch he created, consisting of nothing more than a bumbling old tailor threading a needle—without words, costumes, or props. It became so popular that he performed it to entranced crowds for years. This physical artistry animated his every role. As one critic wrote, "Even the slightest breeze and he is already air-bound."

Zuskin specialized in playing figures like the Fool in *King Lear*—as his daughter puts it in her book, characters who "are supposed to make you laugh, but they have an additional dimension, and they arouse poignant reflections about the cruelty of the world." Discussing his favorite roles, Zuskin once explained that "my heart is captivated particularly by the image of the person who is derided and humiliated, but who loves life, even though he encounters obstacles placed before him through no fault of his own."

The first half of Ala's book seems to recount only triumphs. The theater's repertoire in its early years was largely adapted from classic Yiddish writers like Sholem Aleichem, I. L. Peretz, and Mendele Moykher Seforim. The book's title is drawn from Zuskin's most famous role: Senderl, the Sancho Panza figure in Mendele's *Don Quixote*–inspired work, *Travels of Benjamin the Third*, about a pair of shtetl idiots who set out for the Land of Israel and wind up walking around the block. These productions were artistically inventive, brilliantly acted, and played to packed houses both at home and on tour. *Travels of Benjamin the Third*, in a 1928 review typical of the play's reception, was lauded by the *New York Times* as "one of the most originally conceived and beautifully executed evenings in the modern theater."

One of the theater's landmark productions, I. L. Peretz's surrealist masterpiece *At Night in the Old Marketplace*, was first performed in 1925. The play, set in a graveyard, is a kind of carnival for the graveyard's gathered ghosts. Those who come back from the dead are misfits like drunks and prostitutes, and also specific figures from shtetl life—yeshiva idlers, synagogue beadles, and the like. Leading them all is a *badkhn*, or wedding jester—divided in this production into two mirror-characters played by Mikhoels and Zuskin—whose repeated chorus among the living corpses is "The dead will rise!" "Within this play there was something hidden, something with an ungraspable depth," Ala writes, and then relates how after a performance in Vienna, one theatergoer came backstage to tell the director that "the play had shaken him as something that went beyond all imagination." The theatergoer was Sigmund Freud.

As Ala traces the theater's trajectory toward doom, it becomes obvious why this performance so affected Freud. The production was a zombie story about the horrifying possibility of something supposedly dead (here, Jewish civilization) coming back to life. The play was written a generation earlier as a Romantic work, but in the Moscow production, it became a means of denigrating traditional Jewish life without mourning it. That fantasy of a culture's death as something compelling and even desirable is not merely reminiscent of Freud's death drive, but also reveals the self-destructive bargain implicit in the entire Soviet-sponsored Jewish enterprise. In her book, Ala beautifully captures this tension as she explains the *badkhn*'s role: "He sends a double message: he denies the very existence of the vanishing shadow world, and simultaneously he mocks it, as if it really does exist."

This double message was at the heart of Benjamin Zuskin's work as a comic Soviet Yiddish actor, a position that required him to mock the traditional Jewish life he came from while also pretending that his art could exist without it. "The chance to make fun of the shtetl which has become a thing of the past charmed me," he claimed early on, but later, according to his daughter, he began to privately express misgivings. The theater's decision to stage *King Lear* as a way of elevating itself disturbed him, suggesting as it did that the Yiddish repertoire was inferior. His own integrity came from his deep devotion to *yidishkayt*, a sense of essential and enduring Jewishness, no matter how stripped-down that identity had become. "With the sharp sense of belonging to everything Jewish, he was tormented by the theater forsaking its expression of this belonging," his daughter writes. Even so, "no, he could not allow himself to oppose the Soviet regime even in his thoughts, the regime that gave him his own theater, but 'the heart and the wit do not meet.'"

In Ala's memory, her father differed from his director, partner, and occasional rival, Mikhoels, in his complete disinterest in politics. Mikhoels was a public figure as well as a performer, and his leadership of the Jewish Antifascist Committee, while no more voluntary than any public act in a totalitarian state, was a role he played with gusto, traveling to America in 1943 and speaking to thousands of American Jews to raise money for the Red Army in their battle against the Nazis. Zuskin, on the other hand, was on the JAC roster, but seems to have continued playing the fool. According to both his daughter and his trial testimony, his role in the JAC was almost identical to his role on a Moscow municipal council, limited to playing chess in the back of the room during meetings.

In Jerusalem, Ala told me that her father was "a pure soul." "He had no interest in politics, only in his art," she said, describing his acting style as both classic and contemporary, praised by critics for its timeless qualities that are still evident today in his film work. But his talent was the most nuanced and sophisticated thing about him. Offstage, he was, as she put it in Hebrew, a *"tam"*—a biblical term sometimes translated as fool or simpleton, but which really means an innocent. (It is the first adjective used to describe the title character in the Book of Job.) It is true that in trial transcripts, Zuskin comes out looking better than many of his co-defendants by playing dumb instead of pointing fingers. But was this ignorance, or a wise acceptance of the futility of trying to save his skin? As *King Lear's* Fool put it, "They'll have me whipp'd for speaking true; thou'lt have me whipp'd for lying, and sometimes I am whipp'd for holding my peace." Reflecting on her father's role as a fool named Pinia in a popular film, Ala writes in her book, "When I imagine the moment when my father heard his death sentence, I see Pinia in close-up . . . his shoulders slumped, despair in his appearance. I hear the tone that cannot be imitated in his last line in the film—and perhaps also the last line in his life?—'I don't understand anything.'"

Yet it is clear that Zuskin deeply understood how impossible his situation was. In one of the book's more disturbing moments, Ala describes him rehearsing for one of his landmark roles, that of the comic actor Hotsmakh in Sholem Aleichem's *Wandering Stars*, a work whose subject is the Yiddish theater. He had played the role before, but this production was going up in the wake of Mikhoels's murder. Zuskin was already among the hunted, and he knew it. As Ala writes:

One morning—already after the murder of Mikhoels—I saw my father pacing the room and memorizing the words of Hotsmakh's role. Suddenly, in a gesture revealing a hopeless anguish, Father actually threw himself at me, hugged me, pressed me to his heart, and together with me, continued to pace the room and to memorize the words of the role. That evening I saw the performance . . . "The doctors say that I need rest, air, and the sea . . . For what . . . without the theater?" [Hotsmakh asks], he winds the scarf around his neck—as though it were a noose. For my father, I think these words of Hotsmakh were like the motif of the role and—I think—of his own life.

———————

Describing the charges levied against Zuskin and his peers is a degrading exercise, for doing so makes it seem as though these charges are worth considering. They are not. It is at this point that Hanukkah antisemitism transformed, as it inevitably does, into Purim antisemitism. Here Ala offers what hundreds of pages of state archives can't, describing the impending horror of the noose around one's neck.

Her father stopped sleeping, began receiving anonymous threats, and saw that he was being watched. No conversation was safe. When a visitor from Poland waited near his apartment building to give him news of his older daughter Tamara (who was then living in Warsaw), Zuskin instructed the man to walk behind him while speaking to him and then to switch directions, so as to avoid notice. When the man asked Zuskin what he wanted to tell his daughter, Zuskin "approached the guest so closely that there was no space between them, and whispered in Yiddish, 'Tell her that the ground is burning beneath my feet.'" It is true that no one can know what

Zuskin or any of the other defendants really believed about the Soviet system they served. It is also true—and far more devastating—that their beliefs were utterly irrelevant.

Ala and her mother were exiled to Kazakhstan after her father's arrest, and learned of his execution only when they were allowed to return to Moscow in 1955. By then, he had already been dead for three years.

In Jerusalem that morning, Ala told me, in a sudden private moment of anger and candor, that the Soviet Union's treatment of the Jews was worse than Nazi Germany's. I tried to argue, but she shut me up. Obviously the Nazi atrocities against Jews were incomparable, a fact Ala later acknowledged in a calmer mood. But over four generations, the Soviet regime forced Jews to participate in and internalize their own humiliation—and in that way, Ala suggested, they destroyed far more souls. And they never, ever paid for it.

"They never had a Nuremberg," Ala told me that day, with a quiet fury. "They never acknowledged the evil of what they did. The Nazis were open about what they were doing, but the Soviets pretended. They lured the Jews in, they baited them with support and recognition, they used them, they tricked them, and then they killed them. It was a trap. And no one knows about it, even now. People know about the Holocaust, but not this. Even here in Israel, people don't know. How did you know?"

———

That evening I went out to the Old City again, to watch the torches being lit at the Western Wall for the second night of Hanukkah. I walked once more through the Jewish Quarter, where the oil lamps, now each bearing one additional flame, were displayed outside every home, following the tradition to publicize the Hanukkah miracle—not merely the legendary long-lasting oil but the miracle of military and spiritual victory over a coercive empire, the freedom to be uncool, the freedom not to pretend. Somewhere nearby, deep underground, lay the ruins of the gymnasium where de-circumcised Jewish boys once performed naked before approving crowds, stripped of their integrity and left with their private pain. I thought of Benjamin Zuskin performing as the dead wedding jester, proclaiming, "The dead will rise!" and then performing again in a "superior" play, as *King Lear*'s Fool. I thought of the ground burning beneath his feet. I thought of his daughter, Ala, now an old woman, walking through Jerusalem.

I am not a sentimental person. As I returned to the stone house that night, along the streets lit by oil lamps, I was surprised to find myself crying.

Chapter 5

FICTIONAL

DEAD

JEWS

AS A NOVELIST I AM FORTUNATE TO GET A LOT OF MAIL from readers, some of it more pleasant than others. Years ago, one of my esteemed readers sent me the following email:

Dear Ms. Horn, I recently began reading your book The World to Come *[about a pogrom survivor]. After the scene of the horse being beaten, I threw the book across the room. With all the cruelty in the world, I find it more of a service to mankind to write a book for people to laugh, enjoy and be uplifted. Best wishes, Denise.*

I wrote, but did not send, a reply to Denise:

Dear Denise, Sorry about the horse. It was a reference to Crime and Punishment, *which is another book you might want to avoid. You should also steer clear of the Bible, which is likewise not a great book for people who want to laugh and enjoy. However, I do have some Garfield comics I can highly recommend for their service to mankind. Best wishes, Dara.*

It's easy to laugh at Denise, but her message reveals many readers' unspoken expectations about the purpose of literature. Sophisticated readers don't insist on Garfield and happy endings, but I've found that even educated readers who appreciate tragedy still secretly expect a "redemptive" ending— or as Denise put it, something "uplifting." I've thought about Denise's stupid email to me for many years, because it raises a very fundamental question: What are stories for? That question becomes even harder to answer when we consider that an astonishing proportion of what counts today as "Jewish" literature in English is basically Holocaust fiction. If the purpose of literature is to "uplift" us, is it even possible to write fiction that is honest about the most horrifying aspects of the Jewish past?

When I was in my twenties, I went and got a doctorate in comparative literature just to answer this question. The answer was depressing, for all the wrong reasons.

———

I entered graduate school in order to study Hebrew and Yiddish literature, but the scholars and critics I had to read in the comparative literature department's required courses were all basing their ideas on what I quickly learned were "normal" literatures: English, German, Russian, Spanish, French. That's when I noticed the problem that distinguishes literature in Jewish languages from most other literary canons, and essentially makes Jewish literature into a kind of anti-literature— one that should make everyone question what they want out of a work of literary art.

In 1965, the American literary critic Frank Kermode published his monumental work *The Sense of an Ending*, which essentially tries to explain the purpose of storytelling. Kermode points out how much readers desire coherent and satisfying endings, and then connects that desire to the history of Western religion. He compares literature with religion in what he calls its "desire for consonance," or the desire to live in a world that makes sense. As he puts it, "Everything is relevant if its relevance can be invented." Readers, he says, are like fundamentalists who see everything as a sign from God, because in literature, every detail actually does matter. Just as religion urges us to see our world as an inherently meaningful place where events always serve some larger purpose, writers create that purpose within stories by making every detail add up to something meaningful, thereby inventing a coherent world. As a graduate student who was simultaneously writing novels, I read this and patted myself on the back. See, I wasn't just procrastinating on my dissertation; I was inventing a coherent world!

But I very quickly saw the problem. This idea of religion imposing coherence on the world sounded absolutely nothing like the religion I knew best. Kermode's argument is based on the idea that Western religion is all about "endings." As he puts it, "The Bible is a familiar model of history. It begins at the beginning with the words 'In the beginning,' and it ends with a vision of the end, with the words, 'Even so, come, Lord Jesus.'"

Needless to say, this is not how the Hebrew Bible ends. The Tanakh, as Jews call the Hebrew Bible, has plenty of apocalyptic visions, but its final pages in the rather plodding Book of Chronicles don't exactly end with a bang. Even the Torah, the part of the Hebrew Bible that Jews publicly chant aloud from start to finish every year and then begin reading again, doesn't have much finality to it, other than the expected death of Moses. Instead, the Torah ends with a cliffhanger, stopping just before the Israelites' long-awaited arrival in the Promised Land. The characters never even make it home. It slowly dawned on me that Kermode's idea of religion giving us an "ending" isn't universal at all. It's Christian.

In graduate school, of course, we quickly left Kermode and his contemporaries behind and continued on to structuralism, deconstruction, and other more adventurous schools of thought. But as a writer rather than a scholar, I found that Kermode's idea stayed with me, because it felt true to the expectations of ordinary readers—including my own. The more I considered it, the more I realized just how pervasive, and how accurate, Kermode's idea of literature actually is for English-language readers. Think about what we expect from the endings of stories—not just Denise, but all of us. We expect the good guys to be "saved." If that doesn't happen, we at least expect the main character to have an "epiphany." And if that doesn't happen, then at least the author ought to give us a "moment of grace." All three are Christian terms. So many of our expectations of literature are based on Christianity—and not just Christianity, but the precise points at which Christianity and Judaism diverge. And then I noticed something else: the canonical works by authors in Jewish languages almost never give their readers any of those things.

I was studying modern Yiddish and Hebrew literature, and I began to see that the major works in these Jewish languages almost never involved characters getting saved, or having epiphanies, or experiencing moments of grace. In fact, as I read my way through the foundational works in these literatures, I saw that many of the canonical stories and novels in modern Yiddish and Hebrew literature actually didn't have endings at all.

One major point of entry for modern Jewish literature is the early-nineteenth-century fiction of Rabbi Nachman of Bratslav, a religious leader whose homiletic tales became a baseline inspiration for secular and religious Jewish writers alike. Nachman's stories were important enough to later secular Jewish writers that there are even plays and poems written *about* them, well into the twentieth century; even Franz Kafka was inspired by them and adapted them in his own work. Nachman's stories are fairy tales of a sort, written very much like the stories collected by the Brothers Grimm, which Nachman reportedly read in German with enormous interest. They have many of the same princes and knights and quests and magical agents. What Nachman's stories don't have, though, are happy endings—or any endings at all.

Nachman's story "The Loss of the Princess," for instance, has all the elements of a fairy tale: a banished princess hidden away in an inaccessible castle, a noble knight who sets out on a quest to rescue her, and plenty of riddles to solve and giants to battle on the way. But here's how Nachman's story, narrated aloud to his scribe, ends: "And how he freed her, Nachman did not tell. But he did free her." Another story of Nachman's, "Tale of the Seven Beggars," likewise has all the right fairy-tale elements: spunky orphans who get lost in a forest, and then seven roving beggars with stylized disabilities, a sort of Seven Dwarves, who offer the orphans generosity and wisdom. When the spunky orphans grow up and (of course) get married, each of the poetically disabled beggars provides his own *Canterbury Tales*–style story-within-a-story at their wedding feast. It's all rather conventionally satisfying—except that after the sixth beggar, the story simply stops. The seventh beggar never shows up. These missing endings seem like storytelling failures, but they're entirely deliberate. Nachman was making a religious point about living in a broken and unredeemed world.

As I read my way through modern Yiddish and Hebrew literature, I kept running into this pattern. Sholem Aleichem's *Tevye the Dairyman* stories are familiar to English-language audiences from their Broadway adaptation as *Fiddler on the Roof*. But *Fiddler on the Roof* left out a few details, including Tevye's wife, Golde, dropping dead; Tevye's son-in-law Motl dropping dead; and Tevye's daughter Shprintze drowning herself, none of which would have played well on Broadway. What's even less "uplifting" about the *Tevye* stories is their structure. They're like a TV series where each of Tevye's daughters' marriages is a different episode, and each one is more devastating than the last. But as the series progresses and twenty years pass, Tevye himself never changes. He never learns anything; he never realizes anything; he never has an epiphany or a moment of grace. And he's certainly never rescued or saved. Instead he just keeps enduring, which feels achingly realistic. His great power is that he remains exactly who he always was.

No matter whose work I read among these major Jewish-language writers, I kept running into this problem. The Hebrew Nobel laureate S. Y. Agnon wrote amazing novels that built entire worlds out of centuries of ancient Jewish texts that he brought to life in new and ironic ways, but the best ending you can get from him is that maybe after six hundred pages, somebody dies. The foundational nineteenth-century author Mendele Moykher Seforim wrote novels that essentially introduced stylistic literary sophistication to both Hebrew and Yiddish—but his most famous book, full of surreal and world-altering adventures, ends with the protagonist essentially saying, "And then I woke up." The Yiddish Nobel laureate Isaac Bashevis Singer ended almost every one of his novels not with a resolution but with the protagonist disappearing, whether by running away or by literally locking himself into a closet for the rest of his life. My favorite Hebrew novel of all time, A. B. Yehoshua's 1989 masterpiece *Mr. Mani*, is a fantastically inventive story that moves backwards in time through six generations of a Jerusalem family while tracing the family's recurring suicidal gene—until you get to the end, which is really the beginning, when the enduring mystery of the family's self-destruction "resolves" not with an answer, but with a question, one that casts new light over everything that came before, but which remains unanswered.

These stories, I came to understand, were presenting a challenge to the Western idea of the purpose of creativity. Stories with definitive endings don't necessarily reflect a belief that the world makes sense, but they do reflect a belief in the power of art to make sense of it. What one finds in Jewish storytelling, though, is something really different: a kind of realism that comes from humility, from the knowledge that one cannot be true to the human experience while pretending to make sense of the world. These are stories without con- clusions, but full of endurance and resilience. They are about human limitations, which means that the stories are not end- ings but beginnings, the beginning of the search for meaning rather than the end—and the power of resilience and endur- ance to carry one through to that meaning. Tevye, after griev- ing for his wife, daughter, and son-in-law and being expelled from his home, finally leaves the reader with a line that would never work on Broadway: "Tell all our Jews everywhere that they shouldn't worry: our old God still lives!"

I eventually came to understand the profound insult inher- ent in the messages I was receiving, both directly and indi- rectly, from readers expecting uplifting Jewish literature full of moments of grace—not to me as a novelist, but to

my ancestors who endured experiences like those I gave to
my characters, and in a sense, to all those who have endured
the most atrocious moments of Jewish history. Readers who
demanded that "coherence" from literature about the modern
Jewish experience were essentially insisting that Jewish suffering was only worth examining if it provided, in the words
of my reader's memorable message, "a service to mankind."
In retrospect I am stunned by how long it took me to understand just how hateful this was. Consider, as I only very slowly
did, what this demand really entails. Dead Jews are supposed
to teach us about the beauty of the world and the wonders of
redemption—otherwise, what was the point of killing them
in the first place? That's what dead Jews are for! If people were
going to read about dead Jews, where was the service to mankind I owed them?

This is far from a fringe attitude among contemporary
readers, as just about every bestselling Holocaust novel of our
current century makes fantastically clear. Holocaust novels
that have sold millions of copies both in the United States and
overseas in recent years are all "uplifting," even when they
include the odd dead kid. The Tattooist of Auschwitz, a recent
international mega-bestseller touted for its "true story," man-
ages to present an Auschwitz that involves a heartwarming
romance. Sarah's Key, The Book Thief, The Boy in Striped Pajamas,
and many other bestsellers, some of which have even become
required reading in schools, all involve non-Jewish rescuers
who risk or sacrifice their own lives to save hapless Jews, thus
inspiring us all. (For the record, the number of actual "righteous Gentiles" officially recognized by Yad Vashem, Israel's

national Holocaust museum and research center, for their efforts in rescuing Jews from the Holocaust is under 30,000 people, out of a European population at the time of nearly 300 million—or .001 percent. Even if we were to assume that the official recognition is an undercount by a factor of *ten thousand*, such people remain essentially a rounding error.) In addition to their wonderful non-Jewish characters, these books are almost invariably populated by the sort of relatable dead Jews whom readers can really get behind: the mostly non-religious, mostly non-Yiddish-speaking ones whom noble people tried to save, and whose deaths therefore teach us something beautiful about our shared and universal humanity, replete with epiphanies and moments of grace. Statistically speaking, this was not the experience of almost any Jews who endured the Holocaust. But for literature in non-Jewish languages, that grim reality is both inconvenient and irrelevant.

What does a novel about the horrors of Jewish history in a Jewish language look like?

For English-language readers drowning in uplifting Holocaust fiction, here is one novel, among many, that demonstrates a more honest way to write fiction about atrocity: Chava Rosenfarb's *The Tree of Life*, a panoramic Yiddish-language trilogy about the Łódź Ghetto. To call it a masterpiece would be an understatement. It is the sort of work—long, immersive, engrossing, exquisite—that feels less like reading a book than living a life.

Make that ten lives. That's about how many major characters

we come to know intimately in Rosenfarb's sweeping epic, and we meet them all in vivid detail before the war begins, so we know who they are before sadists take over their lives. Some are sadists themselves, like Mordechai-Chaim Rumkowski, the infamous Nazi-selected "King of the Jews" who ruled the Łódź Ghetto with an iron fist; we first meet him before the war, as an orphanage director who sucks up to rich donors while sexually molesting his young female wards. Most are "ordinary" people—except there's no such thing as ordinary, as the vast variety of the Jews of Łódź makes clear. Prewar Łódź was one-third Jewish, and Rosenfarb brilliantly unfolds a panorama of the city in all its diversity by intertwining her complex characters' lives. The wealthy industrialist Samuel Zuckerman is obsessed with the history of the Jews of Łódź, an interest he shares with Itche Mayer, a poor Jewish carpenter in his employ—and into whose slum neighborhood Zuckerman himself moves when that slum becomes the ghetto. Zuckerman's family-man civility is disdained by Adam Rosenberg, another wealthy industrialist in his circle who thrives on cruelty and sexual conquest. We meet rationalists like the doctor Michal Levine, proud Polish patriots like the spinster teacher Dora Diamant, passionate Communists like the orphaned Esther, Socialists and Zionists among Itche Mayer's sons, and the slightly surreal "Toffee Man," a religious father of nine who periodically appears unbidden, offering other characters unexpected moments of hope. Nor are these characters reducible to representatives of a type or class. They are each embedded, as real people are, in networks of families, lovers, friends, and enemies; each is inspired by their own commitments and also plagued by private doubts. The integrity of these characters depends, as it does for all of us, on their inherent adulthood, their agency in their own choices. In the ghetto, none of that disappears; each character remains exactly who he or she was before, just in inhuman circumstances. The Holocaust was not a morality play, except perhaps for its perpetrators. And that's exactly what makes the ghetto's horrors real.

I would have thought these horrors would be impossible to convey, except that Rosenfarb brings you there. Despite our own culture's saturation in violent imagery, *The Tree of Life* is extremely difficult to read. There is no ruminating about God here, no contrived conversations with Nazis that show their humanity, nor even any brave rebellion—at least, not until the very end. Instead there is confusion, starvation, denial, and sheer sadistic horror. As you read, you are shocked to realize that no one in the book knows what you know. Instead they believe, when imprisonment and forced labor commence at the start of Volume Two, that this slavery and starvation is the central atrocity they are enduring. When deportations begin, some even opt in, reasoning that things cannot possibly be worse. It is only when familiar and sometimes bloodstained clothing begins returning to the slave-labor processing centers (in some cases with family photographs still in the pockets) that some characters realize what is happening—yet even they are quickly (and gladly) silenced by the forces of denial. Meanwhile, German soldiers shoot children in the streets for fun. Power politics among "influential" Jews quickly becomes a blood sport, with people stopping at nothing, including

sexual servitude, to protect themselves and those they love—
all, of course, to no avail. Soon characters we care about begin
falling like dominoes, whether deported, starved, diseased,
shot, or tortured; one major character winds up castrated. By
Volume Three, the Germans demand that the Jews hand over
all children under ten.

Rosenfarb herself (1923–2011), a renowned Yiddish poet who
lived most of her life in Canada, survived the Łódź Ghetto and
subsequently Auschwitz and Bergen-Belsen. *The Tree of Life*,
published in Yiddish in 1971 and in English translation in 1985,
could be mistaken for a survivor's testimony. The extreme
detail with which Rosenfarb brings to life Jewish Łódź, its
people and its passions, is itself an enormous achievement, a
monument and a memorial to a destroyed community, written in the great (and alas, very long) tradition of Jewish literary lament. Yet *The Tree of Life* is not a work of testimony
but a work of art. One character, the aspiring teenage poet
Rachel Eibushitz, most closely resembles Rosenfarb herself,
but this character is simply one of many and hardly the most
important. Instead of memoir, Rosenfarb offers true imagination, bringing us into the minds of many different people and
rendering even the most despicable figures with the utmost
imaginative empathy.

Yet the greatest miracle for the reader is the chance to
meet the city's artists, who come to life in Rosenfarb's words.
One of the novel's most vivid characters is the poet Simkha
Bunim Berkovitch, Rosenfarb's stand-in for her own poetic
mentor Simkha Bunim Shayevitch, who was murdered at
Dachau after the murders of his wife and two young children.

Berkovitch comes from a large Hasidic family, but loses his faith as he discovers his poetic talent. A poor factory worker, Berkovitch is a true artist, living only to create; his life means nothing to him without the ability to produce his poetry, and his only fortune in the ghetto is a menial job he obtains (with help) that allows him time and space to write. It's a drive all writers can understand. One of the book's most affecting early scenes involves Berkovitch's marriage to a woman who ultimately can't appreciate his art. A lesser novelist would play up this conflict, but Rosenfarb knows that artists are humans who live with contradictions. The uncompromised beauty of Berkovitch's family life is among the startling wonders of this novel—and its sudden destruction is among its most devastating.

Amid the unrelenting horror, Rosenfarb's characters render miracles. In one of the book's most astonishing scenes, a group of young people and another poet gather in the street, drawn by the poet's humming of a classical symphony; the poet leads them to the tiny room of Vladimir Winter, a middle-aged hunchback introduced as "the Rembrandt of the ghetto." The young people crowd the room, its walls covered with brown paper, as Winter orders the poet to recite his work. As he recites, Winter takes a box of crayons and begins illustrating the words, covering the walls with surreal drawings that incorporate the men and women in the room, imposing their faces on animals, casting their bodies into open meadows, dipping their hands into pools of water, winding their hair into clouds. When the poet finishes reciting, Winter continues drawing as the light fades outside, and one young woman begins to sing, continuing the creative trance. When all four walls are covered, the poet turns on the electric light and the visitors rise from the floor, looking around as if "falling into a dream. There was a land surrounding them, a land of painful beauty, of light and shadows, which enveloped them with the perfume of an unknown life." Winter then passes out from tubercular fever. The book's last volume ends—or rather, stops—at the gates of Auschwitz. It does not provide an inspirational quote.

That "unknown life," of course, was the creative worlds lost by the murders of these artists; Rosenfarb's work itself, for all its power, can only hint at their destroyed potential. For them there is no redemption except in this novel's pages—a redemption only possible through us, the readers. But we as readers cannot ask the book to uplift us, the way we expect, obscenely, for every other book about atrocity. Reading this monumental work requires an active commitment. It provides, one might say, a service to mankind: it broadens your life beyond your own imagining, allowing your life to include many other lives within it. It brings you down to the deepest level of existence, and offers what Rosenfarb herself describes in a poem called "Praise":

> When the light fades
> And the end approaches
> And abruptly you see yourself standing
> In a deep dark gate
> Look back one more time
> At that bubble of reality,

And praise it, that day
That drips out from being—
Unnoticed,
Vanished,
In the night of forgetting.

Chapter 6

LEGENDS OF DEAD JEWS

AMERICAN JEWS ARE A HIGHLY EDUCATED GROUP OF people—and not just educated, but great at asking annoying questions. In the most recent Pew Survey, 49 percent of American Jews claimed that a key part of their Jewish identity involved "being intellectually curious." In other words, American Jews see themselves as people who don't merely value their university degrees, but also their skepticism, their critical-thinking skills, and their refusal to take anything at face value.

So I didn't think it was a big deal a few years ago when I gave a public lecture at a Jewish institution and casually mentioned that the family story so many American Jews have heard, that their surnames were changed at Ellis Island, is a myth. At Ellis Island, which has been up and running as a National Park Service museum for over thirty years, this is routinely announced on public tours. More recently, we have entered an era of trendy genealogy, bolstered by cheap DNA testing that has led tens of thousands of Americans down the rabbit hole of ancestry research, with ample guidance from online forums, TV documentaries, family tree construction software, and accessible archival databases. With this public glut of information, I hardly thought my mention was news.

Wow, was I wrong.

After that talk, I was mobbed by people—angry people, in a scrum. These were well-read, highly educated American Jews, each of whom furiously explained to me that while maybe *most* people's names weren't changed at Ellis Island, *their* great-grandfather was the exception. None of these people offered any evidence, other than to assure me, "My great-grandfather wouldn't lie!"

I didn't lose any sleep over my Ellis Island mob. But then it happened again. I wrote an article for a Jewish publication in which I compared the "My name was changed at Ellis Island" story to similar historical material, such as Washington chopping down the cherry tree, the CIA killing Kennedy, and the lunar landing being faked to impress the Soviets. In the comments section, hundreds of people explained to me how I was totally wrong, because . . . well, instead of evidence, they then inserted a five-hundred-word anecdote about their great-grandmother, *so there.*

My angry hecklers have taught me a great deal about the power of founding legends, about mythmaking and its purpose.

But now I know I have to get the facts out of the way first. So, for the record: No, your family's name was not changed at Ellis Island, and your ancestors were not the exception. Here is how we know.

First of all, there was no language problem at Ellis Island. Immigration inspectors there were not rent-a-cops. These were highly trained people who were required to be fluent in at least three languages, and additional translators circulated to ensure competency—and in this context, the languages spoken by Jewish immigrants were far from obscure. Second, immigration processing at Ellis Island wasn't like checking ID at today's airports. These were long interviews, twenty minutes or more, because the purpose of this process was to weed out anyone who was likely to become, in the jargon of the time, "a public charge." So this was not a situation where some idiot behind a desk was just moving a line along.

Even if it were: *nobody at Ellis Island ever wrote down immigrants' names*. Immigrants' names were provided by ship's manifests, compiled at the port of origin. Ships' manifests in Europe were based on passports and other state-issued documents. Those compiling ships' manifests were very careful to get them right, because errors cost them money and potentially their jobs. Any immigrant who was improperly documented on board these vessels had to be sent back to Europe at the shipping company's expense.

Yet there is ample evidence of name changing: thousands of court records from the 1920s, '30s, '40s, and '50s of Jewish immigrants and their children filing petitions in New York City Civil Court in order to change *their own* family names.

In her book *A Rosenberg by Any Other Name*, the historian Kirsten Fermaglich tracks these court filings. For legal name changes, petitioners had to provide the court with their reasons for changing their names. And that's where we see the heartbreaking reality behind the funny stories about Ellis Island. In these legal petitions, as Fermaglich unemotionally reports, we meet thousands of American Jews, most of them born in the United States, explaining under oath that they are changing their names because they cannot find a job, or because their children are being humiliated or discriminated against at school, or because with their real names, no one will hire them for any white-collar position—because, essentially, American antisemitism has prevented their families' success.

In her analysis of thousands of name-change petitions, Fermaglich notes many clear patterns. One is that those with Jewish-sounding names overwhelmingly predominated such court filings. In 1932, for instance (nearly a decade after the closure of Ellis Island), over 65 percent of name-change petitions in New York were filed by people with Jewish-sounding names. The next-largest group, those with Italian-sounding names, made up a mere 11 percent of filings. Granted, the Jewish population of New York that year was twice the size of the city's Italian American population—but not six times the size. Another pattern Fermaglich uncovered is that petitioners with Jewish-sounding names often filed name-change petitions *as families*; frequently the motivation cited for the name change involved the educational and professional prospects of the petitioners' children. In these petitions that Fermaglich rather dispassionately describes, we witness ordinary

American Jews in the debasing act of succumbing to discrimination instead of fighting it.

American antisemitism during the decades that followed the mass migration was, as Fermaglich puts it, "private" and therefore "insidious." In the earlier part of the twentieth century, such discrimination was not subtle, appearing in job advertisements with the warning "Christians Only" or at hotels and restaurants posting signs declaring "No Dogs or Jews Allowed." (My childhood piano teacher, a Juilliard alumnus and retired cocktail pianist, once told me how he was hired as a young man in the late 1940s to play the lobby of Florida's prestigious Kenilworth Hotel, where performing musicians were named on lobby signs. As he approached the hotel, he saw the dreaded sign reading "No Dogs or Jews Allowed," and wondered how he, Alan Wolfson, would manage to pass. He soon found himself playing a grand piano beside a marquee the hotel had provided, announcing: "Tonight's Performer: Alain de Wolfe.") By midcentury, these explicit markers had morphed into an elaborate glass ceiling that was an open secret, expressed at first through carefully worded advertising for employment or public accommodations ("sabbath observers need not apply"; "churches nearby") and later through byzantine job and school application forms that, as Fermaglich explains, demanded information not only about the applicant's birthplace and citizenship but also equally mandatory and entirely irrelevant information about the applicant's parents' and grandparents' birthplaces, parents' professions, mother's maiden name, and grandparents' surnames. Fermaglich points out the profound, "corrosive" effect of this type of intense and unacknowledged discrimination on the target population: "The unofficial nature of American antisemitism encouraged many Jews to resist discrimination by using bureaucratic name change petitions to reshape their personal identity rather than civil rights activism to change an unfair society."

Fermaglich is careful to note that the vast majority of Jewish name-changers did not actually take on new non-Jewish identities; most continued contributing to Jewish organizations and participating in Jewish communal life. Fermaglich presents this point optimistically, as a grand refutation of the popular assumption that such people rejected their Jewish roots. But to me, this fact demonstrates just how profoundly oppressive the situation must have been, if even those who chose to participate in organized Jewish communities felt that a name change was necessary. These people were not "self-hating Jews." They were simply staring down a reality that they could not deny. And as the wording of their petitions reveals, they also could not allow themselves to admit exactly what that reality was.

As I pored through Fermaglich's selections from this ream of archival material, what I found most heartbreaking was witnessing how these Jewish name-changers participated in the very humiliation that they were seeking to escape. They did so not merely by changing their names, but by censoring their own self-expression *during the very act of changing those names*—because in their court filings, as Fermaglich reports, virtually no petitioners identified antisemitism as their motivation.

Instead, the Jewish petitioners almost uniformly referred to how their names were "foreign-sounding" or "difficult to spell and pronounce"—even, Fermaglich notes, "when the name was spelled phonetically." "The name Greenberg is a foreign-sounding name and is not conducive to securing good employment," one very typical petition reads. Rose Lefkowitz declared her last name "difficult to pronounce." (Is there more than one way to pronounce "Lefkowitz"?) Louis Goldstein declared his name "un-American, uneuphonius, and an economic handicap"—a petition that was rejected by the judge, whose name was also Louis Goldstein. (Those who beat the odds in an unfair system, of course, are the ones most invested in claiming the system is fair; if they didn't need a workaround, there must not be anything to work around.) Max Hymowitz described how his son Emmanuel found their shared surname "cumbersome" and "an annoyance"; his father felt that changing their name would "substantiate and promote his son's comfort and interests, socially, educationally, economically, and patriotically." One couple, pleading on behalf of their family, testified that "The name of Tomshinsky is difficult to remember and properly spell, and because of this, petitioners and their children have been subject to embarrassment and your petitioners believe that it would be to the best interests of their children as they mature, to have the family name changed to the proposed name of Thomas." In fact, the only petitioners Fermaglich cites whose filings actually mention antisemitism are non-Jews seeking to

change their Jewish-sounding names, so as not to be mistaken for Jews.

Of course, many names circulating in the United States during this period were "foreign-sounding" and "difficult to pronounce and spell"—for example, LaGuardia, Roosevelt, Juilliard, Lindbergh, DiMaggio, Vanderbilt, Earhart, Rockefeller, and Eisenhower. Yet as the remarkably low numbers of non-Jewish name-change petitioners in New York City demonstrate, such families and their forebears do not appear to have been "subject to embarrassment" or affected "socially, educationally, economically, and patriotically" by having names that were "difficult to pronounce and spell." Fermaglich interprets these Jewish petitioners' concealing of the actual problem to mean that, as she gently puts it, "Jews were uncomfortable talking about antisemitism, and may have even been ashamed of their experiences with antisemitism." The difficulty these American Jewish families were facing had nothing to do with spelling or pronunciation, but none of them could admit it. And thus the process of hiding one's name became embedded within the more elaborate process of hiding the reasons why.

This brings us to the reality behind the funny family stories of names that were "changed at Ellis Island." The Ellis Island legend is simply the final step in this multigenerational process of denying, hiding, and burying the reality that American Jews feared most—namely, the possibility that they were not welcome here.

So now we know the myth, and we know the reality. And now we can ask the more interesting questions: Why did so many American Jews' ancestors tell this story about their names being "changed at Ellis Island"? What purpose did it serve then, and why do educated skeptical people still want to believe it now?

Those people who accosted me at my talk and online weren't merely uninformed. They were responding to something enormously powerful and important. This mythological story about the Jews' arrival in America is shared by plenty of Americans from other ethnic groups, immortalized on film in the classic scene of Vito Corleone's arrival at Ellis Island in *The Godfather II*. But it is also part of a deep pattern in Jewish history, one that is much bigger than a single generation of immigrants and their children, one that goes back centuries.

————

Nearly every diaspora Jewish community in world history has at least one founding legend, a story about its origins that members of that community accept as fact, no matter how ridiculous that story might be. The Jews of medieval Spain, for example, in some ways resembled American Jews today, a group that included many people who excelled professionally and politically in the society in which they lived. One of those accomplished medieval Spanish Jews was a twelfth-century man named Abraham ibn Daud. The leading philosopher of his generation, he also had a sideline writing groundbreaking books on astronomy—and in his spare time, he published *Sefer Ha-Qabbalah* (The Book of Tradition), the most widely accepted history of the Spanish Jewish community. In that book is a story about exactly how the Spanish Jewish community became the center of the Jewish world, and the story is so ridiculous that it's amazing that anyone in their right mind ever thought it was true.

Two centuries after the "fact," ibn Daud recounted this origin story: Four important rabbis from Babylonia, the center of Jewish scholarship for centuries, were traveling by ship on the Mediterranean in the year 990—and then, on the high seas, their ship was captured by a royal Spanish fleet. All four rabbis were taken as captives and sold as slaves in different places around the Mediterranean, and in each place, local Jewish communities bought the captives' freedom. One of the captives, Rabbi Moshe, wound up in the Spanish city of Cordoba. One day, the newly liberated Rabbi Moshe, now a penniless refugee, sat in the back of a Torah study class. When he began offering brilliant answers to the class's Torah questions, the community recognized his gifts and made him their new leader. And thus, says ibn Daud, the crown of Torah was transferred from Babylonia to Spain, making Spain the next link in the chain of Jewish tradition.

This story has some truthiness to it, but as the twentieth-century historian Gerson Cohen has thoroughly explained, it's impossible. The story claims that the leader of the royal fleet that hijacked the rabbis' ship was Abed al Rachman the Third. This would have sounded plausible to ibn Daud's readers, since Abed al Rachman the Third really was the king of Spain. Unfortunately, Abed al Rachman died thirty years before this story allegedly took place, among many other factual errors. Nearly every event that "happens" in the story is lifted directly from another source—the medieval version of an internet meme. The story about the unknown pauper

Rabbi Moshe wowing senior scholars in the study session, for instance, is suspiciously similar to a story in the Talmud about the rise of the Roman-era rabbi Hillel the Elder. So why would an obviously intelligent person record this story as official history? And why did centuries of smart Jews in Spain believe it?

One could ask the same question about the founding of the Jewish community in Poland. When the Jews arrived in Poland a thousand years ago, the story goes, the head of the Jewish community announced in Hebrew, *"Poh-lin"*—"Here we will dwell," and that name spread to the local people and stuck. In case that didn't make Poland Jewish enough, the Jews coming to Poland, afraid of persecution in this new land, hid during the day in caves in the Polish forests, studying Talmud. They then sneaked out at night to carve the names of the tractates they were studying onto the trunks of trees. The local Polish people noticed this and began revering these places as holy. Later, Jews who arrived in Poland discovered just how welcome they and their traditions were in this bountiful new land, because the names of all the tractates of the Talmud were already carved onto the trees of the Polish forest, waiting for them.

These ridiculous stories were not only in fashion in the generations following the Jewish migration to Poland centuries ago, but they were also repeated as fact by respected modern Jewish authors—including the wildly popular nineteenth-century Polish Yiddish writer I. L. Peretz, who essentially owned Yiddish publishing for fifty years, and also by the twentieth-century Polish-born Hebrew writer S. Y. Agnon, who won the Nobel Prize for Literature in 1966.

There are endless examples of such origin stories. Jewish communities in France claimed that Jews had lived there since the time of the First Temple in Jerusalem, nearly 3,000 years ago—it's not true, but it was a great alibi for explaining to their Christian neighbors why they weren't involved in killing Jesus. Jewish communities in parts of Algeria similarly claimed they had been living there since the time of the Second Temple, two thousand years ago—also not true (though it was true in other parts of North Africa), but it was a great alibi for telling Muslims that they were already there before the Islamic conquest. One of my favorite founding legends is a story about the very first Jewish "diaspora" community, the Israelites' biblical sojourn in Egypt. Rabbinic tradition claims that one reason the Israelites survived their time in Egypt was that they never changed their Jewish names. But anyone who's ever read the Torah knows that the very first Israelite in Egypt was Joseph, and the book of Genesis explicitly describes how he changed his name to an Egyptian one. Of course, Joseph's name change is nothing compared to the later biblical Book of Esther, in which the title character, who bears the Hebrew name Hadassah, becomes the queen of the Persian Empire and keeps her Jewish identity a secret—helped along by her new name, borrowed from the Persian goddess Ishtar. Jews have been changing their names to non-Jewish ones and lying about it for a long, long time.

———

There's a clear pattern to these legends, which are all about living in places where you are utterly vulnerable and cannot admit it. These stories express the Jewish community's two highest hopes and deepest fears. The first hope is that the Jews in this new place will remain part of the chain of Jewish tradition, and the second hope is that the local population will accept them. The fears, of course, are the inverse—of being cut off from that chain going back to Mount Sinai, and of being subject to the whims of the non-Jewish majority. These fears couldn't be more real, because being a diaspora community means being vulnerable. It is a highwire act of the highest order. There are political strategies for dealing with that vulnerability, but these founding legends are an emotional strategy, and their power is unmatched.

In ways that made sense to each community, these stories each created a fantasy of total acceptance in a non-Jewish setting, and of total continuity with Jewish tradition. In the Spanish story, the enslaved and victimized rabbi survives, untraumatized and unscathed, to become the communal leader—and the chain of Torah scholarship is unbroken between Babylonia and Spain. In the Polish story, the message is that the people of Poland love the Jews so much that they named their country after Hebrew words and even honored their holy texts. This was a fantasy that Polish Jews desperately needed to get them through the far less welcoming reality they lived in.

As minorities limited by sheer numbers in their ability to control the majority's determination of their fate, all diaspora Jewish communities are fundamentally vulnerable. This unforgiving fact also applied to the American Jewish community at the time when 2 million Jews arrived through Ellis Island, and perhaps even more so, to the American Jewish community at the time when those 2 million people's children became adults. Surviving and thriving in this reality required far more than bravery and resilience. It demanded creativity, imagination, and above all, an utterly irrational faith in the fantasy of acceptance. Believing in a fantasy takes conscious effort. It requires convincing oneself of the absolute necessity of believing, and then never relenting, ever.

These new Americans and their children, living in what they hoped was the first place in centuries where their families could enjoy full and free lives, soon discovered that when they applied for a job as Rosenberg no one would hire them, but when they applied as Rose, everyone would. Imagine the private humiliation of changing your name, of accepting the unspoken yet undeniable fact that this intergenerational marker of who you are is publicly considered revolting. Imagine the betrayal: At enormous risk and expense, you or your parents had fled other places to spare yourself and your children this very same humiliation, but now you suffer the slow, seeping, soul-shaking discovery that this new place is, in important and life-limiting ways, no different. Not merely accepting this new and devastating reality, you lie in court about your motivations for succumbing to it—or, even worse, you yourself believe your own lies, because the reality is too painful to acknowledge.

Now imagine telling your children, years later, about what you did.

Telling them the truth wouldn't only implicate you. It would also implicate America. You'd be telling your children that you thought you would be accepted here, but you were fooled, because this place is just like everywhere else—only more insidious, because the discrimination isn't written into the law, so you can't even publicly protest it. All you can do is submit to it, publicly agree with it, announce in court of your own free will that your name is "un-American," that the very essence of who you are is unacceptable. If you tell that story to your children, you'd be confirming two enormous fears: first, that this country doesn't really accept you, and second, that the best way to survive and thrive is to dump any outward sign of your Jewish identity and symbolically cut that cord that goes back to Mount Sinai—which, in the case of names like Levy and Cohen, Hebrew names denoting the descendants of the ancient Jewish priesthood, it actually does.

Now imagine that instead of telling your children these psychologically damaging things, you have another option. You can do what Jews have done for thousands of years, and create an origin story that turns those fears into hopes. You can tell your children that something funny happened at Ellis Island, something completely innocent that didn't hurt you but only helped you. If you tell that story, you've accomplished two things. First you've made America into a place where people maintain their Jewish identity without any interruption of the line from Sinai, and second, you've made America into a place so welcoming that happy non-Jews greet you at the door, and then make innocent mistakes that coincidentally help you to fit right in, at no cost to you or to the three-thousand-year-old tradition you want to maintain. This is the legend that the ancestors of today's American Jews created for their descendants. We were told that our ancestors were definitely not humiliated people facing the reality of American antisemitism, even though that is demonstrated by thousands of court records. No, our ancestors were brave and hopeful people whom America joyously welcomed through that golden door. The lethal attacks on American Jews in recent years have been so shocking and disorienting not merely because of their sheer violent horror, but because they contradict the story American Jews have told themselves for generations, which is that America has never been a place where antisemitism affected anyone's life. We don't simply prefer this founding legend. We need it. The story is more important than the history, because the story is the device that makes meaning.

———

For some people, like my angry readers, it's upsetting to learn that the Ellis Island story is "only" a legend. But I find it empowering, because it reveals the enormous emotional resources available to our ancestors and to us. Our ancestors could have dwelled on the sordid facts, and passed down that psychological damage. Instead, they created a story that ennobled us, and made us confident in our role in this great country—which means we have that creative power too.

We can't change the past, but we can change its meaning. Doing so is an act of creativity, but it is foremost an act of bravery and love. To those who gave us that enduring legend of names changed at Ellis Island, I have only one thing to say: Thank you.

Chapter 7

DEAD
AMERICAN JEWS,
PART TWO

AT THE END OF THE HOLIDAY OF PASSOVER IN 2019, I WAS
full of rage.

This is not how I usually feel after Passover. In my family,
Passover is the holiday we look forward to all year. Inspired
by the tradition of making people in each generation feel
as if they personally were freed from Egyptian slavery, we
act out the story with elaborate costumes, props, and special effects. That year, we even built a neon-painted black-lit
Egyptian palace in our basement, along with four hundred
yards of suspended blue yarn representing the parting of the
Red Sea. It's silly, but it works: my children all feel, viscer-
ally, as if they have left Egypt, that their lives are unfolding
in the Promised Land.

That Passover, however, ended with an unhinged gunman opening fire in a synagogue outside San Diego, killing a sixty-year-old congregant and wounding several others, including an eight-year-old girl—six months after another unhinged gunman did the same thing in a Pittsburgh synagogue, killing eleven.

For most Americans, this was just another dismal news headline. For American Jews, though, it was something much, much worse: a confirmation that the Pittsburgh attack was not a one-off, that our cherished belief in America as an exception in Jewish history might be a delusion.

Most organizations I belong to emailed their members official statements of sorrow after the shooting. But unlike the statements from other groups, the Jewish organizations invariably included long detailed lists of their security protocols, concrete ways to prevent more bullets, reasons 1 through 6 why I shouldn't be afraid to take my children to a synagogue to study or to pray. After Pittsburgh, I knew what to tell my children to comfort them: that this wasn't like those ancient horror stories, that our neighbors love us, that America is different. After that Passover, I no longer knew what to tell them.

Passover has always been frightening. The very first Passover took place during the "night of vigil" before the Israelites fled Egypt when, we are taught, the Angel of Death struck down firstborn Egyptians and passed over the Israelites' homes. Since then, Passover has always been a vigil: For centuries, it has also been a time of antisemitic attacks, from medieval blood libels to modern pogroms to the massacre of thirty people at a Passover Seder in Israel in 2002.

Yet there is something even scarier about Passover than the sheer vulnerability of people gathered at prayer. The Bible's famous call for freedom is "Let my people go." But in the Bible, these words are nearly always followed by another phrase: "so they may serve me." The only purpose of this freedom is to enable the people to voluntarily accept divine laws—laws about welcoming strangers, loving one's neighbors, and accepting responsibility for creating a civic society of mutual obligation. For a nation of former slaves, Jewish tradition teaches, this sudden new agency was dramatic, even terrifying. These people discovered that freedom requires hard work: building a community, supporting the vulnerable, respecting others, educating children.

I'm enraged that I feel the need to apologize for writing about this, but I do: I'm so sorry to take up your time by writing—again—about a measly antisemitic attack where "only" one person was killed and "only" one child now has a leg full of shrapnel. There are so few Jews in the world; even in the United States, we are barely 2 percent of the population, a minority among minorities. Who cares if my children have to grow up praying in a lockdown? Statistically speaking, nothing that happens to Jews should be of any consequence to anyone else.

Except that it is.

Since ancient times, in every place they have ever lived, Jews have represented the frightening prospect of freedom. As long as Jews existed in any society, there was evidence that it in fact wasn't necessary to believe what everyone else believed, that those who disagreed with their neighbors could survive and even flourish against all odds. The Jews' continued distinctiveness, despite overwhelming pressure to become like everyone else, demonstrated their enormous effort to cultivate that freedom: devotion to law and story, deep literacy, and an absolute obsessiveness about consciously transmitting those values between generations. The existence of Jews in any society is a reminder that freedom is possible, but only with responsibility—and that freedom without responsibility is no freedom at all.

People who hate Jews know this. You don't need to read the latest screed by a hater to know that unhinged killers feel entitled to freedom without any obligations to others. Antisemitism is at heart a conspiracy theory, and one appeal of conspiracy theories is that they absolve their believers of accountability, replacing the difficult obligation to build relationships with the easy urge to destroy. The insane conspiracy theories that motivate people who commit antisemitic violence reflect a fear of real freedom: a fondness for tyrants, an aversion to ideas unlike their own, and most of all, a casting-off of responsibility for complicated problems. None of this is a coincidence. Societies that accept Jews have flourished. Societies that reject Jews have withered, fading into history's night.

I don't know what to tell my children about this horror, but I do know what to tell you. The freedoms that we cherish are meaningless without our commitments to one another: to civil discourse, to actively educating the next generation, to welcoming strangers, to loving our neighbors. The beginning of freedom is the beginning of responsibility. Our night of vigil has already begun.

Chapter 8

ON RESCUING
JEWS AND
OTHERS

ONE BALMY WINTER MORNING, I TOOK MYSELF ON A
tour of homes in Los Angeles's Pacific Palisades, cruising
along palm-lined streets called Napoli Drive, Amalfi Drive,
Monaco Drive, and other names evoking the opposite side of
the planet. I was the only tourist. The cartoonish palm trees
among the European names reinforced my irrational fear of
Los Angeles, a city that lacks so many of the things I was
raised to consider normal—like seasons, or aging, or people who reserve the word "historic" for events that occurred
prior to 1982. It is a place without markers of mortality, which
made my tour particularly complicated. Instead of driving
by the homes of the Kardashians, I was looking to solve the

mystery of a group of people saved from the Holocaust by an American named Varian Fry.

Between 1940 and 1941, working out of a hotel room and later a small office in the French port city of Marseille, Varian Fry rescued hundreds of artists, writers, musicians, composers, scientists, philosophers, intellectuals, and their families from the Nazis, taking enormous personal risks to bring them to the United States. Fry was one of only a few American "righteous Gentiles," a man who voluntarily risked everything to save others, with no personal connection to those he saved. At the age of thirty-two, Fry had volunteered to go to France on behalf of the Emergency Rescue Committee, an ad-hoc group of American intellectuals formed in 1940 for the purpose of distributing emergency American visas to endangered European artists and thinkers. The U.S. Department of State, which initially supported the committee's mission, slowly turned against it in favor of its supposed allies in the "unoccupied" pro-Nazi French government—to the point of arranging for Fry's arrest and expulsion from France in 1941. During Fry's thirteen months in Marseille, he managed to rescue roughly two thousand people, including a handpicked list of the brightest stars of European culture—Hannah Arendt, Marcel Duchamp, Marc Chagall, Max Ernst, Claude Levi-Strauss, and André Breton, to name a few. Until recently, I had never heard of Fry, even though it is arguably because of him—and because of his equally brave colleagues, including several other non-Jewish Americans—that these artists and intellectuals not only survived but reshaped the culture of

America. But now I was driving through Los Angeles to see the former homes of some of these rescued luminaries—and to meet a filmmaker who is one of the few living Americans who has heard of Varian Fry.

"We pay tribute to the righteous in order to ignore them. There have been no high-caliber books written about the righteous, no rigorous, critical studies of what made these people do what they did." This is what I was told by Pierre Sauvage, the filmmaker who has spent much of the past two decades working on a documentary about Varian Fry. Bearded and bespectacled in a red polo shirt, Sauvage is convinced that the stories of Holocaust rescuers like Fry should be not merely inspirational but instructional—that by studying these exceptional people, we can learn to be more like them. It's a surprisingly lonely point of view. In 1984, Sauvage helped organize an international conference on the righteous, chaired by Elie Wiesel. "We brought all these righteous Gentiles to Washington," Sauvage recalled. "In the breaks between sessions, the righteous Gentiles were standing around being ignored by the scholars. No one spoke to them, no one engaged them. How can scholars not be fascinated by these people?"

Sauvage is the director (and proprietor) of the Varian Fry Institute, a nonprofit archive of "Fryana," as he calls it. On a warm winter morning in Los Angeles, he welcomed me to the "institute," which turned out to be a small office with floor-to-ceiling shelves of binders that revealed an obsession bordering on mania. Sauvage's collection of Fryana included everything from copies of Fry's letters to textbooks Fry wrote for a public affairs think tank to a poem Fry composed in

French not long before his death. But most of the Fryana was stored on computers, containing video files of what was easily several months of Sauvage's filmed interviews with nearly every person who ever worked with, talked to, knew of, or breathed near Varian Fry.

Sauvage's fascination with rescuers comes in part because he owes his life to them. He was born in 1944 in Le Chambon, France, a Huguenot village in the south central part of the country in which the entire town, following the leadership of its Protestant clergy, formed a silent "conspiracy of goodness," as Sauvage has called it, to shelter Jews from the Nazis. Sauvage's parents were among the thousands of Jews hidden by the righteous of Le Chambon. His 1989 film, *Weapons of the Spirit*, is a documentary about Le Chambon; it has become an educational staple that I watched in my high school French class. Sauvage's parents went to Le Chambon, he later discovered, after being rejected for rescue by Varian Fry.

Fry was honored by Israel's Yad Vashem Holocaust Museum in 1997, thirty years after his death, as one of the "Righteous Among the Nations"; there is also a street named after him in his hometown of Ridgewood, New Jersey, not far from where I live, as well as another street named after him in Berlin. But to Sauvage, this kind of recognition is meaningless when we make no attempt to learn what motivated him. "Many years ago in New York, I read about a guy who had fallen onto the subway tracks, and another man had jumped down to rescue him," Sauvage told me. "When he was asked why he did it, he said, 'What else could I do? There was a train coming.' For most people, that would be the reason *not* to do it. But this man's response was automatic. Fiction and drama have given us a distorted sense of how rescuers think. Writers need a narrative arc, so they show these people wrestling with themselves, agonizing over what to do. But rescuers actually don't hesitate or agonize. They immediately recognize what the situation calls for. When they say that what they did was no big deal, we think they are being modest. They aren't. They genuinely experienced it as no big deal."

From his research in Le Chambon, Sauvage developed his own theory about the righteous: that they are happy, secure people with a profound awareness of who they are. "I've never met an unhappy rescuer," he claimed. "These are people who are rooted in a clear sense of identity—who they are, what they love, what they hate, what they value—that gives them a footing to assess a situation." He described the inspiration the people of Le Chambon drew from their Protestant history and faith. Then he began showing me video footage of his interviews with Fry's colleagues, several exceedingly intelligent, colorful, and sincere Americans. All of them did indeed seem like happy people, with a deep sense of who they were.

The only person missing from his footage is Varian Fry.

I've long been uncomfortable with stories of Holocaust rescue, not least because of the painful fact that they are statistically insignificant—as are, for that matter, stories of Holocaust survival. But for me, the unease of these stories runs deeper. When I was twenty-three and just beginning my doctoral work in Yiddish, I barely understood the world I was entering; it was so distant from American culture, where even stories of the Holocaust are expected somehow to have happy endings.

In Holocaust literature written in Yiddish, the language of the culture that was successfully destroyed, one doesn't find many musings on the kindness of strangers, because there actually wasn't much of that. Instead one finds the overwhelming reality of the unavenged murder of innocents, along with cries of anguish, rage, and, yes, vengeance. Far more palatable to American audiences are stories of Christian rescuers, because while they have the imprimatur of true stories, they also conveniently follow the familiar arc of fiction, inserting heroes into a reality almost entirely populated by villains and victims.

But unlike the humble peasants of Le Chambon, Varian Fry felt oddly familiar to me. Not just because he was young and American, but because he was very much the kind of young American I know best. Like me, he grew up in a commuter suburb in northern New Jersey; he graduated from Harvard in 1931, sixty-eight years before I did. In photographs, he looks a lot like the guys with whom I went to college: thin, awkward, but handsome in a dorky way, his then-stylish glasses and carefully knotted ties a failed but endearing attempt at coolness. His personal letters, which I read in Columbia University's Rare Book Room, are well written and irreverent in a tone I recognize from my college friends—full of witty references to nerdy things ranging from the *Aeneid* ("I was surprised to find so many more / had joined us, ready for exile . . .") to Gilbert and Sullivan ("I am never disappointed in them [the rescued artists]—what never? Well, *hardly* ever!"). If he hadn't been dead for more than fifty years, I might have dated him.

What felt creepily familiar about him, too, were his

motivations. Unlike Le Chambon's pious French peasants, who spoke of living lives worthy of Christ, Varian Fry went to France with a far more secular goal: to save Western civilization. The Emergency Rescue Committee that Fry worked for in France had evolved from an activist organization called the American Friends of German Freedom, a group of prominent American intellectuals from many fields. The Emergency Rescue Committee was formed after France fell to the Nazis, out of the fear that European culture itself was about to be lost forever. American writers, curators, and scholars took great pains to compile an A-list of great brains in need of rescue.

It did not appear to occur to anyone at that time, as premier American minds argued over which premier European minds to include on the list, that there was a sort of eugenics to this anti-Nazi exercise as well——though later it would very much occur to Varian Fry. But when Fry volunteered, it was precisely the mission's elitist nature that excited him. In the introduction to his memoir, titled *Surrender on Demand*, Fry admitted it as one of his main reasons for going to France. "Among the refugees who were caught in France were many writers and artists whose work I had enjoyed: novelists like Franz Werfel and Lion Feuchtwanger; painters like Marc Chagall and Max Ernst; sculptors like Jacques Lipchitz," he wrote. "For some of these men, although I knew them only through their work, I had a deep love; and to them all I owed a heavy debt of gratitude for the pleasure they had given me. Now that they were in danger, I felt obligated to help them, if I could; just as they, without knowing it, had often helped me."

Yet the part of Fry's story that I found most unsettling was that this "debt of gratitude" turned out to be less than mutual. The mystery of why so few people today have heard of Varian Fry—despite his Americanness, his youth, his good looks, his Harvard degree, and the fact that the people he rescued were the guiding lights of Western civilization—seems linked to a peculiar lack of gratefulness among the many famous people whose lives he saved. The stories about how most of these rescued celebrities later avoided or ignored him are numerous and detailed. One of the more glaring examples is Hannah Arendt. Arendt, her mother, and her then-husband were on Fry's lists. As it happened, Arendt and her family left France after Fry's expulsion, saved by the Emergency Rescue Committee's remaining French staffers before the committee itself was shut down by the Vichy police. Yet despite spending a lifetime writing about the philosophical implications of fascism, Arendt never once acknowledged in a single public word that she owed her life to Fry's committee—nor, it appears, in a private one, even when presented with the opportunity. In a collection of letters between Arendt and her fellow public intellectual Mary McCarthy, McCarthy told Arendt about her experience meeting Varian Fry at a friend's home in 1952, describing him as a "perfect madman" and elaborating on that insult in ways both inaccurate and cruel. Arendt replied to McCarthy's letter, but said absolutely nothing in response to the ad hominem attack on the person whose organization had saved her life. Even if Arendt didn't know who Fry was (which would be difficult to imagine, given his immense renown among refugees in Marseille, where Arendt lived while waiting to emigrate to the United States), it is nonetheless remarkable that her Holocaust-related writings, many dealing directly with righteous Gentiles, never mention that she was among the rescued.

Sauvage, who deeply admires Arendt, appeared truly pained when he shared this detail with me. "In one of her letters, Arendt says that 'A writer is his life,'" he said, in the tone of a confessional. "How can you spend your whole life without acknowledging this part of your life? Not one word about Fry, or about the attempt to save a culture of which one were a part?"

It was, indeed, very odd. Because of the people Fry saved, New York became the international center of the postwar art world; because of the people Fry saved, American universities became the premier research institutions on Earth; because of the people Fry saved, Hollywood was reconfigured into global hegemony. Varian Fry, essentially, saved not only thousands of people but the culture of Europe. Weren't we supposed to have seen this movie already?

I asked Sauvage who had been involved in Fry's mission, and he ticked off the various American players who had worked with Fry in France. Every one of them had already died, and Sauvage was the only one who had filmed interviews with them. So I decided to explore the only evidence left, in the hopes of unraveling the mystery of Fry's heroic actions— as well as the darker mystery of why the culture he saved has largely forgotten him. The answers were far more disturbing than I could possibly have imagined.

———

In 1935, Varian Fry was twenty-seven years old, spending a month in Berlin as the editor of the American magazine *The*

Living Age, when he witnessed how a modern civilized country executes a pogrom. Near the end of his trip, storm troopers engineered a riot that happened to take place right outside his hotel. Hearing shouting in the streets from inside the lobby, he stepped out onto the Kurfürstendamm, which at that time was among the city's most expensive and fashionable streets.

"I found a large crowd lined up on both sides of the street, forcing each car which came by to run the gauntlet, stopping all cars in which Jewish-looking men or women were riding, and dragging out the Jews and beating them up," he reported by phone for the Associated Press. "I saw one man brutally kicked and spat upon as he lay on the sidewalk, a woman bleeding, a man whose head was covered with blood. . . . All along the Kurfürstendamm, the crowd raised the shout 'Jude' whenever anyone sighted or thought he'd sighted a Jew. The cry sent the crowd converging on the poor victim, who was asked for his identification papers. If he could not prove himself a good 'Aryan,' he was insulted, spat upon, roughly handled, and sometimes knocked down, kicked, and beaten." Since gore is now routinely depicted in the news, I found it difficult to appreciate the level of brutality Fry was describing when I first read this article in the archives of the *New York Times*, in which it ran on July 17, 1935. It turned out that Fry, or maybe his editors, had understated the violence for the benefit of delicate New York readers, who perhaps preferred a minimum of blood with their morning coffee. Several of those Fry saw being beaten had died of their wounds by the following day.

But what astonished Fry was less the raw cruelty than the

organized spectacle of it. "At times," he reported, "a chant would be raised . . . 'the best Jew is a dead Jew'—precisely like a Christian liturgy, with a leader speaking the lines first and the crowd chanting them over and over again, line for line, after he had finished. Everywhere the people were in a holiday mood; in fact, one German youth said to me, 'This is a holiday for us.' Old men and young men, boys, Storm Troopers, police, young girls of the domestic servant type, well-bred women, some even in the forties and over—all seemed to be having a good time."

The parallels with Christianity that Fry reported for the Associated Press and the *Times*—the liturgical chanting, the sense of a "holiday"—were not the only ones to come up during his stay in Berlin. Mary Jayne Gold, one of Fry's co-rescuers, wrote in her memoir of Fry telling her of another incident he witnessed in 1935 Berlin that later motivated him to return to Europe. "At a café, Varian watched a pair of storm troopers approach the table of a Jewish-looking individual," Gold recalled. "When the poor man reached nervously for his beer, with a quick thrust of his knife one of the storm troopers pinned the man's hand to the wooden table. The victim let out a cry and bent over in pain, unable to move. . . . I think the mental image of that hand nailed to the table beside the beer mug had something to do with [Fry's] decision to go." I read this story and could not help but notice what the hyperliterate Fry had surely noticed himself. He'd witnessed a crucifixion. It was, of course, too gory a tale for the *New York Times*.

Visiting the Nazis' foreign press office the day after the pogrom, Fry was granted an interview with Ernst Hanfstaengl, the Nazis' chief foreign press officer. Hanfstaengl was delighted to speak with Fry, because he and Fry had much in common. Like Fry, Hanfstaengl was an American—and like Fry, he was a Harvard alumnus. Also like Fry, he was passionate about the creative arts: Hanfstaengl was a talented pianist and composer, and in his younger days he had written several popular fight songs for the Harvard football team. In his current job, he had used his talents again, adapting his Harvard fight songs into anthems for the Hitler Youth. Hanfstaengl cheerily informed Fry that there were two groups within the Nazi Party: a "moderate" wing that wanted to expel the Jews, and a "radical" wing, led by Adolf Hitler, that wanted to murder them. Fry's report of this conversation also appeared in the *New York Times*. In 1942, in an article for the *New Republic* titled "The Massacre of the Jews," Fry admitted that "when Hanfstaengl told me, in his cultured Harvard accent, that the 'radicals' among Nazi party leaders intended to 'solve' the 'Jewish problem' by the physical extermination of the Jews, I only half believed him. I learned better in November 1938." The "cultured Harvard accent" of this Nazi leader haunted Varian Fry, but what haunted me were the Harvard fight songs. It would take me much longer to fully understand their implications.

In 1940, what American intellectuals viewed as an "emergency" finally arose. In June of that year, the Germans took over the northern half of France. With the June 14 fall of Paris, which had become a capital for refugee intellectuals, thousands who had fled Germany suddenly found themselves in what Fry would later call "the greatest man-trap in history." These refugees fled Paris (as did much of the city's population) for France's southern "unoccupied" half, where the French government then herded any German nationals they could find—most of whom were Jews or political refugees—into French-run concentration camps, ostensibly to prevent German espionage. When France surrendered to Germany on June 25, the Nazis established a puppet government based in the southern city of Vichy in exchange for complete collaboration with the Nazis. In Article 19 of the armistice terms, the Vichy government agreed to "surrender on demand all Germans named by the German Government in France"—that is, anyone who was on the Gestapo's list, a list that would quickly expand beyond German Jews and anti-Nazi activists to include just about anyone the Nazis didn't like, including many well-known "degenerate" artists. The window for escape from Europe was closing, but the refugees had nowhere to go. Few countries wanted them, even though they were some of the premier artistic, scientific, and intellectual minds of the world. As Herbert Pell, then the U.S. envoy to Portugal, put it, "There is a fire sale on brains here, and we are not taking full advantage of it."

The Emergency Rescue Committee was created in New York the day after the French surrender—at a prescheduled benefit event for the American Friends of German Freedom— to provide emergency visas for prominent refugees and to escort them out of France. Ingrid Warburg, niece of the German Jewish financier Felix Warburg and a well-known patron of the arts, took the reins in developing lists of endangered European artists as well as in raising money for the cause— mainly, as she told Sauvage decades later, from Jewish donors. Curators at the Museum of Modern Art assembled lists of artists thought to be most in danger. The Nobel Prize–winning German novelist Thomas Mann, teaching at Princeton, provided lists of similarly endangered German-language writers; the leaders of various universities compiled their own wish lists of scholars, thinkers, and scientists.

The committee proposed many people for the job of traveling to the "unoccupied zone" and distributing visas to those on the genius lists, but anyone qualified to do it—those with personal connections to the intellectuals to be rescued, or those who had been refugees themselves—would by definition also be in danger. When no one else stepped up, the committee reluctantly said yes to a thirty-two-year-old volunteer, a nobody who had no relevant experience and no qualifications for the job: Varian Fry.

But who was he?

This is a question that confused me—and it seems to have confused Fry too. One could call him a journalist, but that descriptor would be only somewhat true. He worked for several American magazines, but he never held any such job for more than a year or two, barely ever worked as a reporter, and abandoned journalism entirely before he turned forty. One could call him an intellectual, but that also doesn't quite fit, as the term is usually reserved for academics, pundits, or prolific critics, and Fry was none of these. His teaching was limited to high school, and the vast majority of the writing he would publish in his life was for school textbooks or Coca-Cola Company reports. One could call him a lover of the arts, and that is surely true, but it hardly counts as a profession or an identity—and he was not a patron of the arts, except in the sense that he saved artists' lives.

One could call him a WASP blue blood, but that isn't accurate either; while he was certainly a WASP, he had grown up in a comfortable but not terribly wealthy family, with no pedigree to speak of and no fortune to finance his whims.

Pierre Sauvage insists that rescuers "almost uniformly had a role model that influenced them, because if one doesn't have an image of how one should behave in a similar situation, one simply doesn't know what's possible." If Fry had any such person in his life, it was his grandfather, a man who worked for the "orphan trains," a Children's Aid Society operation that collected abandoned children from city streets and exported them to foster homes in the American west. Fry's second wife, Annette, who divorced him two weeks before his unexpected death in 1967, claimed that Fry was very much inspired by his grandfather's work. (She herself was clearly inspired by it; she published a children's book about the orphan trains thirty years after Fry died.) But as I picked my way through Fry's vast personal papers at Columbia University, to which Annette had donated them after his death, I found no mention of this wonderful grandfather who supposedly inspired the greatest act of Fry's life. Andy Marino, who wrote one of the two biographies of Fry published in the past twenty-five years, points to Fry's experience being bullied at the prestigious Hotchkiss boarding school as a defining moment for him; Fry's hazing there, which included being forced to traverse a room hand-over-hand hanging from a scalding steam pipe across the ceiling, supposedly made him drop out. But this life-changing instance of teenage torment isn't something I could find Fry ever mentioning either—and if being bullied in school motivates people toward heroism, there ought to be a whole lot more heroes in the world. And all of Fry's supposed marginalization did not prevent him from graduating from Harvard, where he not only earned a degree in classics but also co-founded a nationally important literary journal, *Hound and Horn*, with Lincoln Kirstein, who later co-founded the New York City Ballet and was an important member of the planning committee for Lincoln Center. The more I learned about Fry, the less I believed that he was a noble loner isolated by his principles. His personal correspondence covers multiple microfilm reels, featuring many, many people. For an outcast, he sure seemed to have had a lot of friends.

After college Fry moved to New York, where he had a job writing *Reader's Digest*–style books on current events for a publisher and think tank called the Foreign Press Association before taking the position at *The Living Age*. At twenty-three, in 1931, he married thirty-one-year-old Eileen Hughes, an editor at the *Atlantic*. Their marriage was childless and, by all accounts, challenging. It became even more difficult when Fry left for France in August of 1940, planning to bike around Provence and bird-watch while delivering visas to the people on the Emergency Rescue Committee's lists. He expected the job to be completed in four weeks. As it happened, he stayed for more than a year.

———

In our current century, it is difficult to appreciate the vast renown of many of the people on Varian Fry's lists, only a few of whom are still household names. Today, for instance, few readers outside of Germany have heard of the German Jewish novelist Lion Feuchtwanger. But by 1940 he was the most widely read German-language writer in the world and, in translation, one of the most widely read writers in the world, period—a fact especially noteworthy because nearly all of his pre-1940 novels deal with explicitly Jewish themes. The book that catapulted him to fame was *Jew Süss*, published in the United States as *Power*, a fictionalized biography of Joseph Süss Oppenheimer, a Jewish financier for Prussian royalty in the eighteenth century. Oppenheimer's sentencing on fraudulent antisemitic charges included hanging and "gibbeting," or the public display of his hanged corpse in a suspended human-size birdcage for six years. Refusing a last-minute conversion that would have averted his death sentence, Oppenheimer died *al kiddush hashem*, in sanctification of God's name, reciting the Sh'ma, Judaism's central statement of faith in one God. Oppenheimer's story had been fictionalized before and was later the subject of a Nazi film, but Feuchtwanger's 1925 version, in which Oppenheimer is a complex figure forced to choose between power and dignity, became an international bestseller. When Feuchtwanger's close friend Sinclair Lewis won the 1930 Nobel Prize for Literature, Lewis declared in his acceptance speech that Feuchtwanger should have received the prize instead.

Having never heard of Feuchtwanger before, I read *The Oppermanns*, one of the few contemporary novels he ever wrote. Set in 1932 and 1933, *The Oppermanns* is the story of four Jewish siblings in Berlin, scions to a successful furniture business founded by their grandfather in the nineteenth century.

As the Nazi influence grows, each family member's sense of self-worth is degraded or destroyed in a dramatic way—from the elder brother, who is forced to surrender the family's firm to a competitor, to the teenage son, who resorts to suicide to end his humiliation at the hands of his high school teacher, to a younger brother, who signs a petition and ends up in a concentration camp, where he is tortured into madness. Ultimately, the close-knit family is scattered across the world as they flee the country they had always considered home. The novel's events are described as taking place at the *end* of "fourteen years of antisemitic incitement" in Germany, tracing back to Germany's devastating defeat in the first World War. The book is full of references to Judaism, including quotations from the Talmud, yet Feuchtwanger's writing is conventional, engaging but not artistic. Today, the story feels familiar, even trite—until one remembers that it was first published, in German, in November of 1933.

In my own novels, I often struggle with the desire to write current events into fiction. Usually I chicken out, too nervous about branding myself politically or making statements I might later regret. If this is how a writer feels in peacetime in the freest of societies, then the courage required to write a novel like Feuchtwanger's when he did is almost unfathomable. I saw a hint of the scope of that courage in the author's note that appears on the book's first page: "After the type of this volume had already been set, a family by the name of Oppermann advised the publisher that Oppermann is a strictly Christian name and that they would, therefore, like to have it avoided that bearers of the name Oppermann be branded before the general public as belonging to a Jewish family. In view of the existing circumstances, the publisher readily understands this attitude on the part of the Oppermann family and herewith advises the readers of this novel of the facts which the Oppermann family wishes to have readily understood."

Reading the delicate wording of this "author's note" is like watching someone balance on a tightrope over a bonfire. Feuchtwanger had spent 1932 in America on a lecture tour; when Hitler came to power, his house in Berlin was confiscated and he was among the first public figures to be stripped of his German citizenship. With his wife, Marta, he went to France, and by 1940 he had landed in a French concentration camp. A photograph of him behind barbed wire moved one of his readers, Eleanor Roosevelt, to offer her support to the Emergency Rescue Committee—support she would withdraw once the State Department began to turn against the committee's work. By the time Fry arrived in France, Feuchtwanger had already escaped from the camp with the help of the American vice consul in Marseille, Hiram Bingham IV, a righteous Gentile from a long line of traveling truth-seekers. (Hirams I and II introduced Christianity to Hawaii; Hiram III discovered the ruins of Machu Picchu.) Bingham had nabbed Feuchtwanger while prisoners were bathing in a river and then disguised him in women's clothes for the trip to Marseille. Fry found him and Marta hiding in Bingham's house; Feuchtwanger was so famous that he was terrified of being recognized on the street.

The internationally acclaimed and similarly bestselling Austrian Jewish novelist Franz Werfel was even more pas-

sionate in warning his readers about the totalitarian men-
ace. His best-known book, *The Forty Days of Musa Dagh*, has
rightly become an enduring classic. As an anti-Nazi novel it
is more coy than *The Oppermanns*, hiding behind a historical
story about the persecution and murder of Armenians by the
Ottoman Turks. In his own author's note, Werfel goes out of
his way to maintain the charade, declaring, "This book was
conceived in March of 1929, in the course of a stay in Damascus" that inspired him to write about "this incomprehensible destiny of the Armenian nation." It was published in 1933
and became a phenomenon around the world. Werfel lost his
citizenship when Germany annexed Austria in 1938, and, like
Feuchtwanger, he fled to France.

For all of Werfel's international fame, he became even
better known through his wife, Alma, who was notorious
among Europe's creative elite. A non-Jew with family connections high in the pre-Nazi Austrian government and a
romantic attraction to fame, Alma Schindler had already broken the heart of the Austrian painter Gustav Klimt before she
turned eighteen. From that humble beginning, she moved on
to Jewish artists, embarking on a lifetime of screwing over
brilliant Jewish men. She dumped Klimt for the prominent
Austrian Jewish composer Alexander Zemlinsky, whom she
subsequently dumped to marry the rather more prominent
Austrian Jewish composer Gustav Mahler. Mahler, besotted,
dedicated the movements of various symphonies to her; her
later control over Mahler's legacy became so intense and dis-
torting that the term "the Alma Problem" is now a concept
in musicology. Alma dumped Mahler in 1910 to marry one

of her few non-Jewish lovers, the Bauhaus architect Walter Gropius—an experience that exiled Mahler to Freud's
couch and, five months later, an untimely death. To no one's
surprise, Gropius failed to meet Alma's standards, and she
dumped him for the artist Oskar Kokoschka (also later saved
by Fry's mission)—whom she subsequently dumped because,
as she told a friend, "Oskar is not a genius, and I only marry
geniuses." Being no genius, Kokoschka took this even harder
than Mahler. He coped by custom-ordering a nude life-size
Alma mannequin, accurate down to the breasts and genitals,
which he dressed in haute couture and lived with for over
a year, dining with it in restaurants and sitting beside it at
the opera. He then threw a party during which he and his
friends smashed wine bottles over the mannequin's head until
it was destroyed. Alma, meanwhile, had already moved on to
genius husband number three, Franz Werfel—to whom she
wasn't faithful either, but who at least earned her a place on
the lists of the Emergency Rescue Committee.

It was at his first meeting with the Werfels that Varian Fry
would realize, as he put it in a letter to his wife, "the shock of
my own inadequacy"—that is, just how over his head he actually was in Marseille.

They met in the hotel where the Werfels were staying, as
Fry mentions in his memoir, "under the name Mr. and Mrs.
Gustav Mahler." When I read this line, I laughed out loud. The
dark comedy routine between the famous and the star-struck
had only just begun.

"Werfel looked exactly like his photographs," Fry wrote,

"large, dumpy and pallid, like a half-filled sack of flour." The half-filled sack of flour was completing a novel, *Song of Bernadette*, the sale of movie rights to which would later buy him a house in Beverly Hills. Meanwhile he and Alma were hiding from death. In a bathrobe and slippers—because really, why bother getting dressed for the person offering to save your life?—he explained to Fry the precise nature of the problem. Thanks to the Emergency Rescue Committee, the Werfels had obtained their American visas at the U.S. Consulate in Marseille. But leaving Vichy France actually required *two* visas—one for the destination country, and the other an exit visa from the French government. The French government would not issue exit visas to persons whom it had promised to "surrender on demand" to the Gestapo; in fact, applying for one was among the more efficient ways to alert the Gestapo to one's presence in Marseille. Alma knew of people who had left France without exit visas by crossing into Spain over the Pyrenees, but no one knew what happened to them once they arrived in Fascist Spain. Should the Werfels apply for exit visas and hope for the best? Or should they risk leaving the country illegally—and if so, how was this half-filled sack of flour going to climb over a mountain range?

"You must save us, Mr. Fry," Franz Werfel pleaded in English, according to Fry's memoir. "Oh, *ja*, you must save us," Alma said casually, and poured them more wine. Reading this, I could almost hear Alma's languid voice—the voice of a jaded celebrity, accustomed to using other people as means to ends. It seemed clear to me, if not immediately to Fry, that the Werfels in their pajamas had instantly recognized the awed young American as their latest hired help. Unfortunately, Fry had no idea how to help them.

After his date with the Werfels, Fry met Frank Bohn, an American who had been sent by the American Federation of Labor to rescue refugees who were labor activists. Bohn already knew the drill. He explained to Fry that he didn't need to go out looking for the people on his lists. Word would spread quickly that an American had arrived with dollars and visas, and they would come to him. Bohn also explained that the only way to get these refugees out of France was through illegal means. Fry's would be an underground operation, with the cover story that it was a humanitarian mission to provide refugees with money while they waited for legal visas— money they desperately needed, as most had had no income source for months. Fry set up shop at the Hotel Splendide and referred to his "office" by the abbreviated name "Emerescue," or in French, "Centre Américain de Secours."

The visa game had complicated rules. The U.S. State Department had authorized special emergency visas, but the American Consulate in Marseille, eager to please its allies in the Vichy government, took its time issuing them. Even refugees who were able to obtain French exit visas often found that by the time they did so, their American visas had expired. Sometimes a third "transit visa" was also required for travel through Spain and Portugal to Lisbon, from where New York sailings departed. Many stateless refugees could not even obtain the necessary papers for travel within France. Refugees with no papers at all, or whose names were well known— true of many on Fry's lists—needed false passports, which

Fry obtained from a disgruntled former Czech consul. One of the first refugees who met Fry helpfully provided him with a map of the French-Spanish border town of Cerbère, where refugees could bypass border patrols by crawling behind a cemetery wall.

Fry hid the map behind the mirror in his room at the Splendide. Within days, he looked outside his hotel room window and saw long lines of terrified refugees, all waiting for him. The hotel concierge was becoming irate. Fry decided to hire a staff. And these were the dead people whom I was able to meet in Los Angeles, courtesy of the many hours of filmed interviews conducted by Pierre Sauvage.

Fry's right-hand man was Albert Otto Hirschmann, a young German Jew who had come to France to study before the war and then enlisted in the French Army, where he invented an identity for himself as a Philadelphia-born Frenchman named Albert Hermant. With the army's defeat, he had become a specialist in all things illegal, making friends with Marseille's gangsters and becoming Fry's chief link to Marseille's underworld, supplying bogus passports and fenced cash. "My advantage," he told Sauvage, "was that I was not easily scared."

To manage the crowds at the door, Fry hired Charlie Fawcett, a wrestler from the American Volunteer Ambulance Corps. Fawcett recalled a Vichy policeman who tried to deter refugees from entering Fry's offices; Fawcett's professional wrestling hold on the man's head ended his interference. Fawcett also found ingenious ways to conceal messages between Marseille and New York. Since the Vichy police censored all telegrams and mail, important information about the mission had to be sent to New York with refugee couriers—in condoms inserted into toothpaste tubes, for example. Fawcett found a way to hide messages in a trumpet and even learned to play a few tunes that didn't require the third valve, where the messages were hidden, in case border guards got suspicious. It worked. "No one takes you seriously when you're holding a trumpet," Fawcett said with a laugh. Working hard at not being taken seriously, he was once asked by a refugee if he were a bachelor. "When I said I was, she said she had two Jewish women for me to marry, to get them out of France," he remembered. "In the end I married six of them."

Another essential employee was Miriam Davenport, a Smith College graduate from a poor family in Iowa who had been studying art on scholarship in Paris when the Nazis took over. "In France I suddenly realized that I had lost my future," Davenport told Sauvage years later. She came to Fry only because she had fled to Marseille with her next-door neighbor Walter Mehring, a German poet who was on Fry's lists. Noticing her knowledge of art, Fry hired her to process the steady stream of refugees who came through his door—to decide who was famous, who was talented, and who was really in danger. "I'm terrible with names," she said, "but at that time I remembered every client's name, because all these people had were their names." When asked why she took the job, Davenport recalled her Christian upbringing. "The Book of Ruth was read to me as a fairy tale," she told Sauvage. "I felt very strongly that these people were my people, and that I had to do something about it."

One of the things she did about it was to approach Mary

Jayne Gold, a young WASP heiress from Illinois whom she had met during the flight from Paris, for funding to expand Fry's A-list to include a B-list. Gold, who had already donated her private plane to the French Resistance, provided more than cash. When four refugees on Fry's list were imprisoned in the Vernet concentration camp, Fry suggested that Gold use "feminine wiles" to persuade the camp's commandant to release them. Gold, who at thirty-one had already had a dozen years' worth of sexual adventures across Europe, was game. When she arrived at the camp, she saw guards filling in graves before she met the commandant and gave him the names of the prisoners she wanted freed. "I tried to be something between sexy and ladylike," she said. It worked: He asked her out to dinner that night, and their agreement was as tacit as it was clear. But that evening she waited in the restaurant for hours; the commandant had stood her up. The following day she went back to the camp. "I asked him, 'What about our date?' He told me, 'Mademoiselle, I assure you I would have rather had dinner with you, but I had to dine with the Gestapo. Your friends will be on the train at noon, on my honor.' It killed me that he had a sense of honor."

One of the strangest things about watching Sauvage's interviews with these brave people is, as Sauvage had told me, how happy they appear. Articulate, warm, witty, and brilliant, they are impossible to dislike. Their age—most were in their eighties when Sauvage interviewed them—makes their happiness seem almost a part of them, a defining feature of who they are, as Sauvage would have it. But as I watched them recall their experiences, often laughing at their antics from their youthful days, I couldn't help but feel as though something were missing. Perhaps it was merely the filter of an interview, or the polite reserve of a generation taught to hide emotions. But as they spoke of a time that was surely full of impossible choices, the horror of imminent arrest, and the devastating reality of being forced to turn away many thousands of people and leave them to their deaths, these genuine heroes gave no signs on-screen that they had been involved in something that didn't have an entirely happy ending. Instead, they seemed to see the whole thing as a fun adventure, free from any anger or regret.

But then I began to wonder if I were the one being fooled.

"We were misfits," Miriam Davenport said of Fry's team. "We didn't fit the pattern of human behavior, of staying out of trouble and keeping your mouth shut." The biggest misfit was Fry himself. Wanting to project an air of authority, he dressed in dapper pinstriped suits each day, with a pressed handkerchief in his pocket and a flower in his lapel, shaking refugees' hands with supreme confidence and sending them off with a "See you in New York." It was a stage act of the breezy American, at a time when Fry's organization was still so under-resourced that he and his staffers, unable to afford their own office space, were holding meetings in the bathroom of his hotel room with the faucets running to avoid being overheard by Vichy spies. Fry's confident persona with his refugee clients was incongruous, both in war-torn Marseille and with the difficult personality his closest associates knew. "One of the secrets of his success," Gold told Sauvage, "was that he was an ornery cuss." As I was starting to realize, Fry had trouble getting along with anyone.

His need to micromanage the mission led Fry to escort the Werfels over the Pyrenees himself. He also took three other refugees: Heinrich Mann, a phenomenally popular anti-Nazi novelist and brother of Thomas Mann; Heinrich Mann's wife, Nelly; and Thomas Mann's son Golo, a renowned historian. The Feuchtwangers would follow shortly along the same route.

To say the refugees were unprepared for the journey would be a massive understatement. Alma Werfel arrived at the train station with seventeen pieces of luggage, all of which she insisted were essential. (Some contained manuscripts of Mahler's symphonies, though most contained her clothes.) For her stealth trek over the Pyrenees, she wore a bright-white dress, which even the least attentive border guard scanning the horizon would be hard-pressed to miss. Heinrich Mann, unaccustomed to the name on his forged documents, had forgotten to relabel his clothes; Fry, gladly playing the part of hired help, picked Mann's monogram out of his hat for him. When they reached the border, Fry and Alma's luggage took a train through the mountains while the refugees traversed them on foot—with the athletically challenged Werfel nearly being carried over the hills by Leon Ball, another American expatriate who worked for Fry. Along with the luggage, the refugees also ditched their old identification papers with Fry on the train. Their noble servant then had to torch them all in the train's bathroom. "The paper burned with an acrid, choky smoke," Fry later wrote, "and not daring to open the door, I had to get down on the floor for air." When the refugees met him at the Spanish border post many hours later, "we almost fell into one another's arms, as though we were old friends who had been separated for years and had met by accident in some strange city where none of us ever expected to be." That warm embrace, I was beginning to understand, was not quite what it seemed.

Not everyone was so lucky. Fry's most famous failure was the literary critic Walter Benjamin. Fry had provided Benjamin with his American visa, as well as a forged passport and a personal escort over the Pyrenees. Unfortunately, the day in September 1940 that Benjamin arrived in Spain was the day Spain decided to close the frontier. (Prior to that, refugees without French exit visas who slipped past French border patrols could present their Spanish transit visas to Spanish border guards a few miles down the hill without comment.) Terrified of turning back, even more terrified of sneaking further into Fascist Spain, and completely convinced that posterity would take note of the crucial manuscripts in his suitcase, Benjamin killed himself on the Spanish border. The suitcase and its manuscripts were discarded by a customs official after his body was found.

Back in Marseille, Fry had acquired an actual office—which the Vichy police soon raided. He decided that a refuge outside the city was necessary. With funding from Mary Jayne Gold's fortune, he rented a large suburban house full of gilded mirrors and taxidermed animals. It was called Villa Air-Bel.

Air-Bel became a haven for refugee Surrealists, who passed the frigid winter of 1940–1941 there with Varian Fry. Occupants included André Breton, poet and founding father of French Surrealism, who decorated the premises with jars of live praying mantises; his wife, Jacqueline Lambda Breton, a dancer and artist; their five-year-old daughter, Aube, whom the Surrealists already lauded as a brilliant painter; Wilfredo Lam, a French-Cuban painter who was Picasso's only protégé; Benjamin Péret, whom Fry described as "the French poet whose verses sometimes read as though they had been copied down from the walls of public toilets"; Victor Brauner, "the one-eyed Romanian painter whose women and cats all had one eye"; and many other writers and artists, nearly all of whom later became fixtures in the American art establishment. On Sundays, the Saint-Exupérys, Henri Matisse, André Masson, and André Malraux would stop by, staging impromptu exhibits and performances.

Under rationing, they nearly starved. As Fry wrote to his father, "If you want to get some idea of what it is like living in France now, drink Postum with saccharine and no milk, eat stale bread without jam or butter, and treat yourself on rare occasions to a slice of an old horse." But when I read this letter, I could see that for Fry, the exotic austerity was clearly part of the fun. And it was a glamorous austerity indeed. The house came with a cook, a waitress, a laundress, a maid, a gardener, and even a barber who shaved the male occupants daily—and while there wasn't much food, there was somehow plenty of wine. The artists in residence played Surrealist games: putting on exhibits by hanging their paintings from trees, making playing-card decks featuring Baudelaire and Freud, and singing long into the night. It was the high point of Fry's life.

Fry's delight in holing up with the stars of the European intellectual establishment did not go over well at home. The State Department made it clear that it would cooperate with its Vichy French "allies" in tracking Fry's illegal activities. The evil of the American government in discouraging desperate immigrants haunts many students of this period, including Sauvage. In fact, Sauvage believes that the reason Fry is so unknown is precisely because he reveals U.S. complicity in the Holocaust. "We live on two myths—that we didn't know, and that we couldn't do anything even if we did know," Sauvage said to me as soon as I sat down in his office. "This is the religion, and it isn't true. We knew plenty and could have done a lot. Varian Fry was a hero, but he was also a maverick who flew in the face of American policy. He shouldn't be allowed to acquit everyone who wasn't with him." There is a painful and undeniable truth to this. When Fry's American passport expired, the American embassy refused to renew it, placing him in mortal danger. The Emergency Rescue Committee in New York, aware that Fry had run afoul of the State Department, also began calling for his immediate return. But Fry refused to leave.

Fry's wife, Eileen, who stayed in New York and acted as his liaison to the Emergency Rescue Committee, had been begging him to return home for months. She also had her own ideas about Fry's mission. In one of her first letters, before Fry had settled himself in Marseille and disabused her of the common notion that France was full of orphans dying in the streets, she wrote, "I did not speak to you about bringing back a French child, which probably seems an absurd suggestion to you at the moment, and of course I don't want you to go around *looking* for one—I just mean that you must be sure to bring one back if you feel that *is* what you want to do with any special one." The idea of Fry bringing back a French child as a kind of souvenir for his childless wife does seem absurd, compared to rescuing Europe's greatest minds. But in fact Eileen's suggestion was not so different from what Fry was actually sent to France to do—to handpick the "special ones" among the refugees who had been deemed worth saving, and, by necessity, to leave the rest behind to nearly inevitable murder.

The inevitability of murder, of course, is the premise of all narratives of Holocaust rescue—and part of what makes me so uncomfortable with them. The assumption in such stories is that the open maw of death for Europe's Jews and dissidents was something like a natural disaster. These stories, in some sense, force us—people removed from that time by generations—to ask the wrong questions, the kind of questions that we might ask about a shipwreck or an epidemic. *Someone* has to die, this thinking goes, and the only remaining dilemma is who will get the last seat on the lifeboat or the last vaccine. But these questions fall short by assuming that the perpetrators were irrelevant. As long as we are questioning the choices that were made, shouldn't we be considering the possibility of the Holocaust not happening at all? If someone was in a position to choose whether to save person A or person B, shouldn't whole societies have been in the position to reject the notion of genocide altogether? Why didn't everyone become Denmark?

The stories of rescuers that we find most satisfying, as Sauvage points out, are those in which rescuers agonize over what they are doing, wondering whom to save; there is a kind of prurient appeal in observing that agony at a distance, which explains the popularity of fictions like *Sophie's Choice* and fictionalizations like the movie version of *Schindler's List*. Sauvage is disturbed by this notion of the anguished rescuer, because it assumes that people cannot possibly be as good as they actually are. But the unarticulated and more disturbing idea here is that rescuers like Fry do not actually call into question the premise that innocent people are doomed to be murdered. Instead, such stories simply reveal that the most righteous people available could do no more than provide, for a tiny number of people, the possibility of remaining alive. In this sense, rescuer stories are the opposite of inspirational. They are stories that make painfully clear everything that might have been.

Sauvage is not merely dismissive of the elitism charge against Fry's mission; he is positively hostile to it. "I think that devaluing rescuers who only do a little bit is a way for the person who does nothing to make himself feel less guilty," he told me. "You judge a mission by what it accomplished, not by what it didn't accomplish."

This is an odd position for Sauvage to take, given that his own parents, non-famous Jews who did not fit Fry's mission of rescuing celebrity intellectuals, were among the thousands of desperate people Fry had to turn down. In this sense, the survival of Sauvage himself, born in Le Chambon after his parents were lucky enough to find someone who said yes to saving their lives, is one of the things that Fry's committee "didn't accomplish." More confusingly, Sauvage also seems to want us to judge America by what it didn't accomplish—while arguing that the exclusive nature of Fry's mission was exactly what made him want to accomplish it.

When I challenged Sauvage on this, he defended Fry along

with his own theory of the righteous. "Altruism is a bogus concept," he said. Most rescuers, according to Sauvage, derived great joy from what they did. "Fry was meeting a deep need within himself. He was an intellectual, and a lover of the arts. He was really helping the people he loved."

It is certainly true that Fry was saving people who felt like family to him. As he put it in one of his many telegrams to Eileen refusing to leave France, COULD NO MORE ABANDON MY PEOPLE HERE THAN COULD MY OWN CHILDREN STOP HUNDREDS HAVE COME TO DEPEND ON ME FOR MONEY ADVICE COMFORT STOP LEAVING NOW WOULD BE CRIMINALLY IRRESPONSIBLE STOP. In another telegram, begging the committee for more time, he put his concerns more bluntly: PLEASE MAKE THEM REALIZE WE HAVE UNDERTAKEN IMMENSE TASK SAVING CULTURE EUROPE STOP.

"We had hardly any money," Miriam Davenport said in one of Sauvage's interviews, describing how she felt when forced to make decisions about who was worth saving. It was one of her few moments on-screen without a smile. "Our money was specifically designated for people whose art had put them in danger. We were helping the people who were in danger because of what they believed." But what, I wondered, did these rescued people believe?

In December of 1940, Vichy police turned up at Villa Air-Bel and arrested Varian Fry, along with several artists and colleagues. Fry managed to burn some address lists and forged passports in the bathroom, but an anti-Vichy doodle by André Breton was sufficient to imprison the entire group in the Marseille Harbor, on a steamship crammed with six hundred prisoners. Fry threw a note for the American consul onto the pier, wrapped in a ten-franc bill. Receiving the message, the consul sent nothing more than a tray of sandwiches. Once the group was arbitrarily freed three days later, Fry found himself tailed by eight plainclothes cops.

Fry continued sending refugees out of France, and the Vichy police began tapping his phone. They arrested several of his French colleagues, and their aggression toward the refugees worsened when Vichy passed its first anti-Jewish laws in 1941. Police ran dragnets in Marseille, arresting every foreign Jew they could find. One of those arrested was Marc Chagall. In high dudgeon, Fry contacted the police and yelled at them for arresting one of the world's greatest living artists. "If the news of his arrest should leak out, the whole world would be shocked," Fry informed them. Half an hour later Chagall was freed. The team rejoiced. But Mary Jayne Gold spotted Fry wiping his glasses, muttering under his breath, "No, we should be able to save them all. Why just the world's greatest painter?" When I read Gold's account of this moment, I saw in it the very first evidence of a crack in Fry's façade. Before this point, he had seemed like one of the happy rescuers of Sauvage's theory and then some, a cheerful servant of the famous. But now something new was happening to Fry, or perhaps he was merely revealed for who he always was: a person blessed, or cursed, with the ability to see what no one else could see.

On August 29, 1941, the Vichy police arrested Varian Fry on behalf of the U.S. government. As the police chief had explained to Fry a few weeks earlier, "You have caused my good friend the Consul-General of the United States much annoyance. Your government and the committee you represent have both asked you to return to the United States without delay." He was warned then that he would be arrested if he did not leave the country on his own. Fry's wife had attempted to ensure her husband's safety by soliciting help from powerful people in America. The only tangible result was a letter from Eleanor Roosevelt: "I am sorry to say that there is nothing I can do for your husband. I think he will have to come home because he has done things which the government does not feel it can stand behind." Fry's entire staff escorted him to the Spanish border, along with the Vichy police. The Vichy government had thoughtfully provided him with an exit visa.

––––––––

When I drove through Beverly Hills in the depths of winter, searching for the house where Franz and Alma Werfel settled, the yards were mobbed by gardeners, tending to grass planted in a desert at the foot of a tectonic cliff. The Werfels' house is on a road like many others in Beverly Hills, lined with fifty-foot palm trees that form a colonnade like a Roman cardo. The street is a kind of movie set, with each house done in a different style—a Tudor, a Spanish mission, a Bauhaus type, an Italian palazzo, all side by side, with gated driveways and intercom systems. I thought of ringing the bell at the Werfels' former home, a large colonial, until I noticed the foot-wide sign on its lawn from the Greater Alarm Company.

Down the hill in Santa Monica, it's clear that not all of Fry's famous clients shared this level of success. Heinrich Mann had crossed the Pyrenees with the Werfels, sharing their joyous escape from doom. But when I arrived at his home, a ground-level apartment in a concrete bloc painted in unpleasant pastel colors, I saw no alarm-company logos. Instead, the door to Heinrich Mann's final home was marked by a large sign that read THIS AREA CONTAINS CHEMICAL SUBSTANCES KNOWN TO THE STATE OF CALIFORNIA TO CAUSE CANCER, REPRODUCTIVE TOXICITY, BIRTH DEFECTS AND OTHER REPRODUCTIVE HARM. I left quickly, as did Mann. Dismayed by his Pacific paradise, in 1950 he accepted a position as the first president of the German Academy of the Arts in Communist East Berlin, just to escape America—though he died in Los Angeles before returning home.

At the end of my tour I drove to Villa Aurora, Lion Feuchtwanger's palatial home in Pacific Palisades, which is open to visitors. The house was a demonstration home built by the *Los Angeles Times* in 1927, modeling the most modern living in the Los Angeles suburbs. It has specially insulated walls, earthquake-protection features, and a living room that converts to a silent movie theater, with an organ for accompaniment. But when the Depression hit, no one wanted an enormous house—and when the Depression lifted, wartime gas rationing made the suburbs undesirable. The Feuchtwangers bought the Spanish-style mansion on the cheap when they arrived in 1940; today it is used as an artists' colony for German writers and filmmakers. Feuchtwanger quickly resumed his pre-exile success and reassembled his thirty-thousand-volume library, which I explored while enjoying his panoramic views of the Pacific. The house's property used to be much bigger, I was told by the young German woman who took me through the villa, but at some point most of the backyard fell off the cliff, leaving behind only a strip of grass on the edge of a precipice. My guide told me this in a bland voice, as though it were perfectly normal for the earth to fall away beneath one's feet. Feuchtwanger, formerly an outspoken Communist, apparently had no doubts about his new home or his sense of self. As I left the villa, I was handed a postcard photograph of a middle-aged Feuchtwanger smiling, posing in his California courtyard with his two pet turtles.

The triumph of the refugee artists in New York is legendary. "Not only was there a new mode of painting developing in New York by the mid-1940s," wrote the art historian Martica Sawin, "but it was emerging among those artists who had the greatest amount of contact with Surrealist émigrés." Artists like Marc Chagall redefined urban spaces with public art around the world; works by Max Ernst, Marcel Duchamp, André Masson, and others entered the permanent exhibitions of major museums. Their students had names like Robert Motherwell and Jackson Pollock.

Even the rescuers themselves went on to enjoy fruitful careers. Hirschmann, Fry's right-hand man and expert in all things illegal, became an architect of the Marshall Plan and a world-renowned economics scholar at Harvard, Columbia, Yale, and Princeton. Miriam Davenport worked for Albert Einstein's Emergency Committee on Atomic Energy, exhibited as a sculptor and painter, and eventually earned a doctorate in French literature. Charlie Fawcett, Fry's police-wrestling doorman and ace messenger, went to Hollywood and acted in more than one hundred movies, at one point starring opposite Sophia Loren.

But Varian Fry, if he had lived to be interviewed by Pierre Sauvage, would probably not have been smiling. His life after his return from France was not a story of success. He could barely keep a job or a wife. He worked for a time at the *New Republic*, but resigned when he became more anti-Communist than his fellow traveling journalists. He later worked for other publications, but could never get along with a boss well enough to avoid being fired. Leaving journalism in a principled huff, he bought a small TV production company and ran it into the ground. He took a job writing corporate literature for Coca-Cola, but was fired for insisting that Pepsi's drink dispensers were more effectively illuminated. He took a job teaching Latin at an Episcopal school, but was fired for playing his classes a recording of Tom Lehrer's "Vatican Rag." Lucy Frucht, a relief worker who had been in awe of Fry's commanding presence in Marseille, told Sauvage how disoriented she was when she ran into Fry in New York in the 1950s, making cigarette commercials. "In Marseille, he was God," she said. "And then suddenly he was nobody."

His personal life was worse. His marriage to Eileen dissolved almost immediately upon his return from France in 1941. His second marriage, to a much younger woman named Annette Riley in 1952, lasted longer and produced three children, but was difficult long before it ended. Annette, who for decades took charge of Fry's papers and legacy thanks to the fact that Fry did not amend his will in the two weeks between his divorce and his death, insisted in her interviews with Sauvage that Fry was happy in his postwar life. "Guys who came back from the war didn't talk much about it," she told Sauvage. "I do not get the feeling that he was living his life pining after the glory days. He used to say to me that he wanted to be a regular guy and learn about baseball." But Fry went through extensive psychoanalysis and even participated in Alfred Kinsey's study on human sexuality. To his children, Fry was a distant father at his best, and he was not often at his best. His daughter still refuses to speak of him. Ultimately the Fry family's attempt at a suburban postwar idyll could not endure the vagaries of Fry's restless soul. He had thrived in the knife-edge world of wartime Marseille, but what he could less easily endure was what Auschwitz survivor Gerda Weissmann-Klein once described as every concentration camp inmate's abiding fantasy, and the title of her 2004 memoir: *A Boring Evening at Home*.

Behind Fry's angst was something far more profound than the boredom of a war hero living out his days behind a picket fence. He was genuinely anguished over the fate of the thousands, even millions, whom he had been forced to leave behind—and in his anguish I saw what was missing from Sauvage's interviews with his smiling colleagues decades later. "I have tried—God knows I have tried," Fry wrote in his memoir's unpublished preface, "to get back again into the mood of American life. But it doesn't work. . . . If I can make others see it and feel it as I did, then maybe I can sleep soundly again at night." After his expulsion from France, he tried in every way he could to continue fighting. He tried to enlist in the army, but an ulcer kept him out. The Office of Strategic

Services, the CIA precursor that had run covert operations in Europe during the war, didn't want him either; his work in Marseille had involved too many contacts with possible Communists. He then tried screaming his head off about what was happening in Europe. In 1942, he wrote a cover story for the *New Republic* titled "The Massacre of the Jews," reporting with hard evidence on the murders of over 2 million Jews in Europe. "There are some things so horrible that decent men and women find them impossible to believe," he wrote. "That such things could be done by contemporary western Europeans, heirs of the humanist tradition, seems hardly possible." He pleaded for the one thing he knew would have saved the Jews of Europe: offering them asylum in the United States. His plea was roundly ignored, to the tune of 4 million more murders. He then devoted himself to writing *Surrender on Demand*, his memoir, in the hope that it would bring more attention to those he had abandoned in Europe. But the war had been won by the time it was published, and the book received little attention. Americans wanted to hear about their own heroism, not about their failures.

What was perhaps most painful for Fry after his return from France was the dissolution of his relationships with the artists and intellectuals he had saved—or, rather, the revelation that these relationships were themselves a sort of fiction.

Franz Werfel, whom Fry had personally escorted out of France, refused to return Fry's wife's phone calls on Fry's behalf while Fry was still in Marseille. Walter Mehring, the celebrated German poet who had been not only Fry's client but also a personal friend of Fry and his staff, settled in Los

Angeles and signed a lucrative contract to write screenplays for Warner Bros. Fry's committee had advanced him 30,000 francs to establish a new life in the United States. Refugees were not expected to pay back such loans, but Mehring's deadbeat status became harder to swallow when he began cruising around Pacific Palisades in a pricey new convertible while Fry's committee was still scrounging for money to save more lives. When Fry found a publisher for his memoir, his former client Lion Feuchtwanger wrote him a complimentary note: "Your narrative of the events is so impressive that the reader can't help experiencing them with you." But the narrative was apparently not impressive enough for the world-famous author to offer Fry any help getting the book reviewed or read, or even a blurb for the jacket. Their personal correspondence begins and ends with that congratulatory note. Feuchtwanger's lack of gratitude toward Fry's mission actually dated back to 1940, when he first stepped off the boat in New York. At the pier, he began giving interviews in which he thoroughly detailed his escape from France, down to the route he took over the Pyrenees. The risk this posed for Fry's committee's safety, along with that of Feuchtwanger's fellow refugees, can hardly be measured. But Feuchtwanger couldn't have cared less. Soon he would be living in a model home built by the *Los Angeles Times*, with his wife and turtles.

The refugees' ingratitude became painfully clear in 1966, the year before Fry's death. That year Fry decided to raise money for the International Rescue Commission—a philanthropic group loosely evolved from Fry's Emergency Rescue Committee—by putting together a fundraising album of original lithographs from the artists the committee had rescued. Fry thought this would be simple; after all, he had saved these people's lives.

It wasn't.

Reading Fry's papers from that year is an enraging experience. Nearly every page involves some frustrated effort to convince refugee artists to support the group that had saved their lives. There are endless telegrams and letters back and forth in 1966 and 1967 between Fry and Chagall, Fry and Chagall's agent, and Fry and Chagall's second wife, all of whom provide various excuses as to why the renowned artist was unfortunately unable to provide Fry with the time of day. Chagall, whom Fry had not merely supplied with a visa but even personally sprung out of jail when the French police were about to hand him over to the Gestapo, finally did agree to provide a lithograph—but refused to sign it, deliberately reducing its value by orders of magnitude. Fry asked André Breton, with whom he had lived at Air-Bel along with Breton's wife and young daughter, to write an introduction to the album. No amount of begging could convince Breton to do it. In a letter to a friend, Fry tried to justify the failure of so many artists to respond to him: "Artists don't answer letters, usually, if they even read them; and the telephone is no substitute for physical presence—repeated physical presence." He began searching for funding for a trip to France. After seeing Max Ernst's show at New York's Jewish Museum, Fry begged Ernst to participate, eventually yelling at him by mail, I DO NOT WANT THE ALBUM TO COME OUT WITHOUT SOMETHING FROM YOU IN IT!

Ernst would ultimately have even more reason to be grateful to Fry. As I read through Fry's maddening correspondence from 1966 and 1967, the last two years of his life, I came across an incident that I had not seen reported anywhere else. In 1966, a German newspaper published an article claiming that Ernst, who was not Jewish, had deliberately abandoned Luise Straus, his Jewish ex-wife and the mother of his son, to the Gestapo—while he trotted off to fame and fortune in America. In reality, Ernst had offered to remarry Straus for visa purposes, despite being involved with Peggy Guggenheim at the time. Fry was concerned that a fake marriage by the likes of Max Ernst would endanger the whole rescue operation, but in the end he was willing to try it. The only unwilling party was Luise Straus, who preferred taking her chances with the Nazis to remarrying Max Ernst. (She died in a Nazi prison camp.) When Fry heard of the smear against Ernst, he went to tremendous lengths to clear the artist's name. I saw how Fry had dug up copies of the receipt for Luise Straus's American visa, and then how he had solicited affidavits on Ernst's intentions from the former U.S. consuls and vice consuls, from the curators of the Museum of Modern Art in New York, and from witnesses who had been with them in Marseille. But Ernst still largely rebuffed Fry's requests for a lithograph, capitulating only when Fry arrived in France in September of that year to beg him in person. The stress of pleading with Ernst and many other artists during his trip to Europe became so severe that it landed Fry in a French hospital with his first heart attack.

Part of this ingratitude was mere celebrity vanity. As Fry once wrote to his wife, "Mrs. Guggenheim says Chagall is a shit. (Jewish ladies are *so* outspoken!) I guess she's right." But the lack of graciousness was not unique to celebrities. Pierre Sauvage, recalling his research in Le Chambon, pointed out to me that many of those rescued declined to even acknowledge their rescuers in later years. This was partly because they simply wanted to forget the greatest horror of their lives.

But there is also something inherently shameful in the rescuer-rescued relationship—the humiliation of being reduced to depending on another person for survival—and that shame expresses itself in resentment toward rescuers. "Gratitude is what makes you hate someone," Hannes Stein, a German Jewish journalist with whom I shared my bafflement about the legacy of Varian Fry, told me. Stein argued that this type of resentment was completely natural, and he offered his own country as a prime example. "Germans hate America," he went on. "They have three reasons to be grateful to America: America saved them from themselves, rebuilt their country after the war, and saved them from the Soviets. And that's exactly why Germans hate America." If we are honest, we must admit that there is a profound shame in the fact of the Holocaust from the Jewish point of view as well—and I wondered if my discomfort with rescuer stories came directly from that shame. How on earth, Fry's rescued Jews and dissidents must have wondered, could we wildly successful adults have gotten ourselves into this pathetic situation—where our lives suddenly depend on the religious commitments of a pig farmer, or the intellectual ambitions of an oddball like Varian Fry?

The shame is only highlighted by the enormous difference in the experience for the rescuers and the rescued. For those rescued, it was the worst time of their lives, when their lives had the least significance. For the rescuers, it was the best time of their lives, when their lives mattered most. Everyone Fry saved had been living a nightmare. Yet as he left France, Fry wrote to his wife, "I have had an adventure—there is no other but this good Victorian word—of which I had never dreamed."

That good Victorian word, and the literature it evokes, brought me back to the question raised for me when I'd read Fry's *New Republic* article on the massacre of the Jews, in which he marveled that such atrocities could be committed by the "heirs of the humanist tradition." It was to preserve that very tradition, of course, that Fry had gone to France—to, as he put it, SAVE CULTURE EUROPE STOP. As I peered into the chasm between rescuers and rescued, I saw that there was something equally strange about this grand goal of saving Western civilization. What, after all, did that "humanist tradition" consist of? What were its greatest achievements, its highest values? What did those rescued intellectuals actually believe? And when Fry was trying to save European culture, what was he trying to save?

———

Searching for answers, I looked to the writings of one of the Emergency Rescue Committee's biggest success stories, Hannah Arendt—and realized that I had somehow managed to reach adulthood without ever reading *Eichmann in Jerusalem: A Report on the Banality of Evil*, the book for which Arendt is best remembered. Amazed by this gaping hole in my education, I read it on my flight to Los Angeles, and then read it again on my way home. Based on Arendt's reporting for *The New Yorker* on the trial of the high-ranking Nazi, the book is most famous for its assertion of how "banal" the accused appeared, that Eichmann was not a cackling evil genius but rather a boring bureaucratic man, and that this sense of tedium was itself the Holocaust's prime novelty of horror. I knew this before opening the book; more than half a century later, this insight has become almost banal itself. But Arendt's chief argument in that book, I discovered, is actually to convince her readers that the source of Eichmann's—and by extension the Nazis'—evil was Eichmann's "inability to think." "He was genuinely incapable of uttering a single sentence that was not a cliché," she writes, and later elaborates: "He *merely*, to put the matter colloquially, *never realized what he was doing.* . . . It was sheer thoughtlessness—something by no means identical with stupidity—that predisposed him to become one of the greatest criminals of the period."

Yet Eichmann as Arendt describes him, spewing clichés at his trial, did not appear to me at all as a person with an "inability to think." He seemed rather like the opposite—that is, someone who had spent a rather astonishing amount of time thinking, absorbing ideas and translating them into action. It was just that he had been thinking about bullshit, and in the process had become buried so deep in it that extraction had become impossible. Arendt did refine this idea in her later writings, but as I read and reread this book in my airless middle seat on my cross-country flights, I found myself wondering why it was so important to her to claim that Eichmann wasn't capable of thinking. What if he were?

Arendt also claims that the premise of Eichmann's trial in Jerusalem, where he was tried not only for crimes against humanity but for "crimes against the Jewish people," was fundamentally flawed, because for the Jews, as Arendt put it, "the catastrophe that had befallen them under Hitler . . . appeared not as the most recent of crimes, the unprecedented crime of genocide, but on the contrary, as the oldest crime they knew and remembered." Arendt calls this "the misunderstanding at the root of all the failures and shortcomings of the Jerusalem trial." But I couldn't help wondering if the Petliura pogroms in Ukraine in 1919–20, in which more than fifty thousand Jews were murdered in an explicit attempt at genocide, hadn't looked incredibly unprecedented; or if the vast totalitarian brainwashing of the Inquisition, as it used creative rhetoric to convince people to turn their Jewish neighbors in to be burned at the stake, hadn't seemed impressively novel at the time; or if the populist innovation of the Roman Empire, turning the torture and murder of rabbis into public stadium-filling spectacles, didn't strike a philosopher or two as "the most recent of crimes." I thought of more examples like this—two or three per century, just off the top of my head—but it soon became tedious, and I bored even myself. "Evil" may or may not be banal, but killing Jews sure is.

I finished Arendt's book wishing I had liked it—and worried that my failure to appreciate her perspective was a reflection of my own "inability to think." I went to my local library and read a collection of her essays titled *Responsibility and Judgment*, which was on the shelf next to Ayn Rand's *The Virtue of Selfishness*. In her 1971 essay "Some Questions of Moral

Philosophy," Arendt reflects on the disappearance of morality in Nazi Germany: "All this collapsed almost overnight . . . as though morality suddenly stood revealed in the original meaning of the word, as a set of mores, customs and manners, which could be exchanged for another set. . . . Did we finally awake from a dream?"

As I returned the book to its place beside *The Virtue of Selfishness*, I recalled that the American Yiddish poet Yankev Glatshteyn had thought the opposite: For those who had been awake enough, there had never been any dream at all. Born in Poland in 1896, Glatshteyn was a secular man, and American enough to have enrolled in law school at New York University. In his searing April 1938 poem "A gute nakht, velt" (Good night, world) he wrote:

> Good night, wide world
> Big, stinking world.
> Not you, but I slam the gate.
> . . . .
> Go to hell with your dirty cultures, world.
> . . . .
> Flabby democracy, with your cold
> compresses of sympathy.
> Goodnight, electric impudent world.
> Back to my kerosene, tallowed shadows,
> . . . .
> To my pages inscribed with the divine name, my biblical
>   books,
> . . . .

To judgment, to deep meaning, to duty, to right.
World, I step with joy toward the quiet ghetto light.
Good night. I'll give you a parting gift of
   all my liberators.
Take your Jesusmarxes, choke on their courage.
Croak over a drop of our baptized blood.

. . . .

From Wagner's idol-music to wordless melody, to humming.
I kiss you, cankered Jewish life.
It weeps in me, the joy of coming home.

This poem has haunted me since I first read it as a twenty-year-old student at Harvard—a place, I slowly came to understand, that could teach me many things, including how to think, but that could not teach me goodness. Not because it taught the opposite, but because moral education is simply not what secular Western education or secular Western culture is for.

Varian Fry, my fellow alumnus, had noticed this too. When he'd interviewed the Nazi press official Ernst Hanfstaengl in 1935 in Berlin, he was alarmed to discover that Hanfstaengl saw him as a fellow Harvard man. An American with German parents, the clearly bright Hanfstaengl graduated from Harvard College twenty-seven years before Fry and later earned a doctoral degree. Like many Harvard-educated children of immigrants, Hanfstaengl decided to return to his parents' native country in its time of trouble in order to improve it, to do the most good he could with his education. He soon became a personal friend of Hitler's and rose to the level of chief foreign officer at Joseph Goebbels's Ministry of Propaganda. The American had done well for himself, and for his parents' country.

In 1934, a year into his job as head of Hitler's foreign press department, the Harvard Alumni Association appointed Hanfstaengl vice marshal at Harvard's commencement for his twenty-fifth class reunion—in recognition of his achievements as a high-ranking official overseas. Though Hanfstaengl declined the honor after much controversy, he did attend his reunion, trailed by dozens of reporters and a security squad of local and state police. The Nazi regime's attitudes were no secret by 1934; 1,500 protesters met him at the dock in New York. But at Harvard, the sanctity of free intellectual inquiry prevailed, along with hallowed respect for diversity of opinion. The *Harvard Crimson* urged the university to give him an honorary degree. When Hanfstaengl withdrew from the vice-marshalship, he made up for it by donating $1,000 to the university as a "Dr. Hanfstaengl Scholarship," for students to spend a year in the new Germany. In his letter to Harvard president James Conant accompanying his donation, Hanfstaengl wrote, "It is my profound conviction that my years at Harvard have since given me incalculable advantages, not the least of which consist in a knowledge of America and the world and in the spirit of discipline and fair play."

According to the Fry biographer Andy Marino, Hanfstaengl opened his 1935 interview with Varian Fry by asking after their shared alma mater, and then bragging to Fry that the Führer himself enjoyed hearing him play "Three Cheers for Harvard" on the piano. Who wouldn't give three cheers for Harvard, after all—a place where few people, no matter how enormous their other faults, could be accused of Arendt's morally damning "inability to think"? Then Hanfstaengl told Fry that he and the other Nazi moderates were hoping to do the humane thing and export the Jews to Madagascar, while Hitler's faction of more radical Nazis planned to murder them all. When Fry concluded the interview, Hanfstaengl presumably offered his best wishes to the best minds in America, asking Fry to give his regards to their fellow Harvard men.

———————

One problem with Pierre Sauvage's theory of the righteous— that they are happy individuals with a deep sense of who they are—is that it doesn't describe Varian Fry at all. With the powerful exception of his time in France, there don't appear to be many periods in Fry's life when he was "rooted in a clear sense of identity"—or even simply happy.

When I challenged Sauvage on this in his office in Los Angeles, he was defensive, even irritated. "I really believe that when you read Fry during the war years, he does embody that sense of self-knowledge and happiness," Sauvage insisted. "I think it's absurd to suggest that Varian Fry in Marseille wasn't the very embodiment of self-knowledge, of confidence, of knowing he was where he should be."

It is certainly true that Fry was supremely happy and confident in Marseille. But there is something tautological about claiming that the traits that foster righteousness can be expressed only in a situation involving righteous conduct, and they can be painfully absent during the remainder of one's life. How relevant can such traits be, then, if we really want to learn from the righteous—to cultivate their traits in ourselves or to value these traits in others, as Sauvage is so eager for us to do? What really makes a person become a Varian Fry?

Not long after my return from Los Angeles, I spoke with Varian Fry's son Jim. Jim Fry is an evolutionary biologist and the proprietor of his father's papers. When I mentioned Sauvage's idea of rescuers being motivated by a deep sense of who they are, Jim Fry laughed. "When I think of my father," he said, "I don't think of someone who was secure in his sense of self."

Jim Fry was only nine years old when his father died, but I asked him for his impressions of his father, both from his own memories and from those of others who had known him. "He was a difficult person," he began, but clarified: "My father was mentally ill, and struggled with that his whole life. If he were alive today, he'd probably be diagnosed with high-functioning bipolar disorder."

Jim Fry is convinced that his father's mental illness was not something that he developed in middle age, but that he had struggled with it for most of his life, since long before his work in Marseille. He pointed to his father's departure from Hotchkiss, which biographers have made into a bold stand against hazing, and his yearlong suspension from Harvard, which, as his father told it, was solely because of a prank he pulled by putting a For Sale sign on the president's house. "Something about these stories doesn't add up," Jim Fry told me. "He was always alienating people, having weird outbursts."

In one of Sauvage's interviews, Miriam Davenport recalled some of Fry's wackier antics—like receiving visitors in his boxer shorts—and said that she felt Fry was influenced by the screwball comedies of the 1930s. Yet the more I read about Fry, the more apparent it seemed that no such influence was necessary. The memoirs and biography of Lincoln Kirstein, the Harvard friend (and future New York City Ballet founder) with whom Fry created the *Hound and Horn* literary journal, paint a picture of someone whose personal troubles long preceded the war. In his diaries, Kirstein recalled a party at Harvard during which Fry "went nuts," ripping a telephone out of the wall and throwing it out a window. (This seemed innocuous to me at first, until I realized that we were talking about a 1920s institutional wall-mounted telephone—the kind made of cast iron and wood.) The episode was far from unique; the frequency of such incidents led to Fry's suspension from school.

Kirstein's diaries also make it abundantly clear that Fry was gay—something that nearly everyone in Fry's life seems to have known, though the pieties of the era prevented nearly anyone from admitting it. In Marseille, it was obvious enough that even the Vichy police, trying everything to entrap Fry, sent both girls and boys to seduce him. I was raised in an era with its own silly pieties, so just as Annette Fry felt obligated to insert a notice into the papers at Columbia insisting that her husband wasn't "foppish," I feel obligated to make one of the two currently pious claims about an important figure's homosexuality: either that it was irrelevant to his heroism and that considering it relevant makes one a bigot, or that it was the fundamental influence in creating his sense of empathy for others. Neither of these is really true. Instead, Fry's sexuality seems like yet another aspect of his personality—like his intense intelligence, and also like his mental illness—that made it impossible for him to lead a conventional life. And if one believes Pierre Sauvage's claim that the righteous are people who are rooted in an unshakable sense of their own identity, then the mental double life led by the twice-married Fry, and the torment he put his wives and children through in its service, would hardly seem to be a recipe for righteousness.

Fry was sounding less and less like Sauvage's man jumping onto the subway tracks, the one so anchored in the world that he considers risking his life to save someone else to be no big deal. When I asked Jim Fry what motivated his father to take on the rescue mission, his answer did not conjure up anyone resembling the humble peasants of Le Chambon. "I'm sure some of it was a desire to be important and to hang out with famous people," he said. "There were genuine humanitarian reasons, too, but there was a synergy between those reasons and the desire to hang out with famous people and to be recognized for it. My mother has said that he would never admit this, but the year he spent in Marseille was the best year of his life. I can imagine that he was on a manic high the whole time."

Yet something about the manic side of Fry's personality crossed the boundary from troubled into visionary. "As my mother would say, he didn't suffer fools gladly," Jim Fry said. He mentioned his father's resignation from the *New Republic* as an example of his father's "theatrical breaches with people." Fry had quit the magazine in a rage over his fellow editors' refusal to condemn Stalin during the war. "In hindsight," Jim Fry mentioned, almost as an afterthought, "he was right."

That rightness gave me pause. It was the same rightness that Fry exhibited in Berlin in 1935, when the rest of the world was looking for ways to compromise with Hitler; the same rightness that took him to Marseille; the same rightness that wouldn't let him leave. Perhaps Fry actually was, as Mary McCarthy wrote, "a perfect madman." To perceive the blinding irrational vastness of absolute evil, one almost needs to be mad.

When I asked Jim Fry for his own version of what makes a righteous person like his father take the risks that he took to save others, his answer was equally unsteadying. "Maybe you need to be a little unhinged to do something foolhardy like that," he said. He added with a laugh, "If Prozac had existed in the 1920s, we wouldn't be having this conversation."

Then, in a quieter tone, he told me: "What I think is most interesting is how someone so troubled could have done something so valuable and important." He read me his favorite quote about his father, from a review of Andy Marino's biography by Christopher Caldwell: "Fry was impossible to work with, mentally troubled, locked in himself," Caldwell wrote. "But let us not forget that he was a prophet, too, and put himself in harm's way to prevent the future he saw unrolling before him. Not the ideal person, maybe. But certainly the kind that every generation has always had too few of."

Fry may have been a "misfit," as Miriam Davenport put it—a trivial word often used for artists and the other thinkers Fry saved. But artists and thinkers at least know that Western culture honors their kind of work. Indeed, Western culture views them as the guardians of civilization, as the Emergency Rescue Committee did. There is no such cultural assumption, among "heirs of the humanist tradition," about righteousness. It is considered unremarkable, banal. It is not considered what it actually is: prophecy.

Varian Fry's oddness was not that of a Marcel Duchamp. It was that of an Ezekiel. The real reason that no one today has heard of Varian Fry is because the gift he had is not one that we value.

It is easy to forget that there are other values a culture might maintain, other people whom one could consider guardians of civilization instead of artists and intellectuals— and that a large proportion of the people who were actually murdered in the Holocaust adhered to one of these alternatives. Fry tried to save the culture of Europe, and for that he should be remembered and praised. But no one tried to save the culture of Hasidism, for example, with its devotion to ordinary, everyday holiness—or Misnagdism, the opposing religious movement within traditional Eastern European Judaism, whose energy in the years before the war was channeled into the rigorous study of *musar*, or ethics. Entire academies devoted to the Musar Movement were destroyed, their books burned out of the world, their teachers and leaders and scholars murdered—all the things that everyone feared would happen to the vaunted culture of Europe. No rescue committee was convened on behalf of the many people who devoted their lives and careers to what Pierre Sauvage laments that

no one pursues—the actual study of righteousness. For them, there were no Varian Frys.

I returned from Los Angeles in the depths of a frigid winter night, coming home to the warm, dim nightlights of my children's rooms. My five-year-old had papered my refrigerator with incomprehensible drawings to honor my return. I thought of Aube Breton, the five-year-old budding Surrealist with whom Fry once lived at Air-Bel, who now sells her father's papers at auctions for enormous sums. My own five-year-old's work surely could never compare. Yet on the long, dark flight home from Los Angeles, as I took part once more in the obscenely false game of wondering who should have been saved, I could not help wishing that instead of an emergency rescue committee saving Europe's greatest artists, that there had been an emergency rescue committee saving Europe's greatest prophets—that perhaps what should have been saved was not more of the culture of Europe, but more people like Varian Fry.

––––––––

On the morning of September 13, 1967, Varian Fry failed to appear at his new job at a high school in Connecticut, where he had recently been hired to teach Greek and Latin—his greatest love, the foundation of European civilization. When he didn't answer his telephone at home, his former wife Annette, who had divorced him two weeks prior, received a phone call. She immediately contacted the Connecticut State Police, who sent an officer to knock on his door.

The policeman found Fry sitting in bed with his glasses on his lap, his sheets and blankets covered with typewritten pages from his autobiography. He was revising it for an abridged school edition, which was later published under the title *Assignment: Rescue*. He had suffered another heart attack, this one fatal. He was fifty-nine years old.

The police officer noted the contents of the manuscript scattered around the bed, detailing Fry's valiant attempt to save the culture of Europe.

"It appeared," the policeman reported, "to be a work of fiction."

Chapter 9

DEAD JEWS
OF THE
DESERT

ON A NARROW STREET IN DAMASCUS, SYRIA, THE OLDEST
city in the world, I pull open a heavy iron door in a cinder-
block wall and enter an ancient synagogue. Behind the door,
just past a tiled courtyard shaded by a large tree, I step inside
and am stunned by what I see.

I'm standing in a jewel box. The small room is illuminated
by dozens of elaborate beaded chandeliers; its walls are covered with thick red velvet drapes, its stone floor with richly
patterned carpets. In front of me is a large flat stone topped
with a golden menorah: Here, an inscription informs me,
the Hebrew prophet Elijah anointed his successor Elisha, as
described in the biblical Book of Kings. (Legend dates this
synagogue to biblical times, though historical sources confirm

its age at a mere five hundred years.) For a place that drew Jewish pilgrims for centuries, it is remarkably well preserved—and startlingly intimate. There are no "pews" here; instead, there are low cushioned couches facing one another, as though this were a sacred living room. A raised marble platform at the room's center has a draped table for public Torah readings; on the room's far end is an ornate wooden cabinet filled with ancient Torah scrolls, their parchments concealed inside magnificent silver cases. On the walls are framed Hebrew inscriptions, featuring the same prayers my son is currently mastering for his bar mitzvah in New Jersey. I read the familiar ancient words and feel my breath leave me with the jerking motion of a dream, tripping on a missing step as I fall through a hole in time.

I should mention here that I've never been to Damascus. Also, this synagogue no longer exists.

I'm on the website of a virtual museum called Diarna, a Judeo-Arabic word meaning "our homes." The flagship project of the nonprofit group Digital Heritage Mapping, Diarna is a vast online resource that combines traditional and high-tech photography, satellite imaging, digital mapping, 3-D modeling, archival materials and oral histories to allow anyone to virtually "visit" Jewish historical sites throughout the Middle East and North Africa, though the project has now expanded to include sites around the globe.

As I write this, with the coronavirus pandemic trapping millions of people in quarantine, virtual tours have become de rigueur for hundreds of international tourist attractions. Diarna might seem like just one more online field trip, a fun way to hop on a screen and explore. But Diarna is something entirely different from a digital playground: It is an outrageously difficult and utterly thankless effort in preserving places that apathy and malevolence have almost erased from the world. The places Diarna documents aren't merely threatened by political instability, economic hardship, authoritarianism, and intolerance. In many cases, Diarna's virtual records are all that stands between these centuries-old treasures and total oblivion. That synagogue I "visited," the Eliyahu Hanavi-Jobar Synagogue in Damascus, was documented by one of Diarna's photographers in 2010. In 2016, Syria's civil war transformed the priceless five-hundred-year-old site to rubble—photos of which you can also find on Diarna. The implications of this project are enormous, not only for threatened Middle Eastern minorities, but for everyone. It has the power to change the very nature of how we understand the past.

Diarna was created in 2008 by Jason Guberman-Pfeffer, who was then a recent college graduate active in Middle Eastern human rights circles, and Fran Malino, a Wellesley professor (now emerita) studying North African Jewish history. That year, a mutual acquaintance of theirs traveled to Morocco to explore her family's Moroccan-Jewish roots, and she found that many of the places she visited—synagogues, schools, and cemeteries—were startlingly decayed. And the elderly people who remembered the places best were dying off. At that point, the senior scholar Malino and the young activist Guberman-Pfeffer put their heads together and realized that by combining their archival skills, their contacts in the region, and newly available technologies, they could create, in the virtual world, a way to preserve these places forever.

"It morphed almost immediately into this huge project," remembers Malino, who is now Diarna's head of Digital Heritage Mapping. Malino began by recruiting among her own students, but was soon startled by how many young people—including American photographers and budding scholars, and also locals in the region—signed on. "In very short order with a very small budget, we had a number of people working for us so we could set up a website and accumulate a lot of information and photos."

Over a decade later, with Guberman-Pfeffer as its director, Diarna has run more than sixty field expeditions, sending photographers and researchers to collect information and visual evidence of the remains of Jewish communities in dozens of countries, and the organization has now documented nearly three thousand sites throughout the Middle East and North Africa, as well as elsewhere in the world. On Diarna's online interactive map, anyone can zoom in and explore them all. Some of these locations include little more than a town's name and basic information about its Jewish history, with research still in progress. But many include beautiful photography showing physical sites from many angles, bibliographies of historical resources, and oral histories from former Jewish residents describing lives lived in these places. Other sites are being elaborately documented in ways unimaginable even just a few years ago. Today, Diarna's photographers and researchers are using tools like a portable no-parallax camera that creates a fully immersive 360-degree view of a building's interior, drone photography for bird's-eye views of ancient ruins, and design software that can turn traditional photography into vivid 3-D models.

Social media has also made it newly possible, even easy, to collect amateur photos and videos of places otherwise inaccessible, and to locate people who once lived in these Jewish communities. Diarna's interactive map often includes links to amateur videos and photos when no others exist, giving people a window on sites that are otherwise invisible. And as former Jewish residents of these places age beyond memory's reach, Diarna's researchers are conducting as many in-person interviews with such people as they can, creating a large backlog in editing and translating these oral histories to make them accessible to the public. "We're in a race against time to put these places on the map," Guberman-Pfeffer says, "and to preserve these stories before they're forever lost."

I've been thinking about time and loss since I was six years old, when it first dawned on me that people who die do not ever return—and that this was also true for each day I'd ever lived. My obsession with this unforgiving fact turned me into a writer, chasing the possibility of capturing those disappearing days. These efforts inevitably fail, though I stupidly keep trying. When I first learned about Diarna, I was a bit alarmed to discover an entire team of people who not only shared my obsession, but who were entirely undeterred by the relentlessness of time and mortality—as if a crowd of chipper, sane people had barged into my private psych ward. The bright, almost surreal hope that drives Diarna is the idea that, with the latest technology, those lost times and places really can be rescued, at least virtually, from oblivion.

Jews have lived throughout the Middle East and North Africa for thousands of years, often in communities that long pre-dated the Islamic conquest. But during the mid-twentieth century's tumultuous power shifts in the region between colonial and postcolonial control, political instability and anti-semitic violence intensified to create a vast exodus, driving nearly a million Jews to emigrate to Israel and elsewhere, leaving entire countries all but devoid of Jews—and leaving behind synagogues, schools, and cemeteries that served these communities for generations. The circumstances of this mass migration varied. In some places, like Morocco, the Jewish community's flight was largely voluntary, driven partly by spo-radic antisemitic violence but mostly by poverty and fear of regime change. At the other extreme are countries like Iraq, where Jews were stripped of their citizenship and had their assets seized, and where, in the capital city of Baghdad, a 1941 pogrom left nearly two hundred Jews murdered and hundreds of Jewish-owned homes and businesses looted or destroyed.

Today, people and governments in the region have vary-ing attitudes toward the Jewish communities that once called them home. Morocco publicly honors its Jewish history; there, the government has supported Jewish site maintenance, and Diarna cooperates with a local nonprofit called Mimouna (named for a Moroccan-Jewish post-Passover celebration), a group devoted to documenting Jewish life. In other places, there is public denigration or even denial of a Jewish past. In

Saudi Arabia, for instance, decades of pan-Arabist and Islamist propaganda have left the public ignorant that Jews even lived in the kingdom at all after the Islamic Conquest, despite recent official efforts to recognize the kingdom's remarkable Jewish historical sites, including the ruins of entire Jewish cities.

Diarna is officially apolitical, refusing to draw conclusions about any of this—which for a novelist like me is maddening. I want the past to be a story, to mean something, especially a past as dramatically severed from the present as this one is. So do lots of other people, it turns out, from Zionists to Islamic fundamentalists. Guberman-Pfeffer politely declines to engage. "It's not our job to give a reason why this particular village doesn't have Jews anymore," he tells me. "We just present the sites." Malino, as a historian, is even more rigorous in defending Diarna's neutral approach. "In my mind the goal is to make available to all of us, whether they're in ruins or not, the richness of those sites, and to preserve the wherewithal of accessing that information for the next generation. We are not taking a political position, not trying to make a statement. Absolutely not."

Every Diarna researcher I talked to stood firm on this point. But the choice to present these Jewish sites is itself a statement, one that underscores an undeniable reality: "The Middle East is becoming more homogenous."

I hear this from Diarna's chief research coordinator, Eddie Ashkenazie, himself a descendant of Syrian Jews, who emphasizes the project's value for people in the region today. "We're pointing out that the store next to your grandfather's in the market was once owned by the Cohen family," he says.

"Whether they got along or it was fraught with tension is going to vary depending on the time and place, but it testifies to a society that had other voices in it, that had minorities in it, that was heterogeneous. Today you have whole societies that are only Libyan Muslims, or only Shi'ite Arabs. But they used to be incredibly diverse. All Diarna is trying to do is say that Jews once lived here."

Diarna is currently focused on documenting Jewish communities in rural areas of North Africa and the Middle East, where establishing this simple historical reality is a radical act. "We are rewriting the history books," Ashkenazie claims, and then corrects himself: "Or, not rewriting; we're just writing this history, period. Because no one else has yet."

Ashkenazie walks me through an elaborate presentation that spells out exactly how Diarna does its current work. He tells me about the Libyan town of Msellata, where a former Jewish resident, interviewed by one of Diarna's researchers, mentioned that the synagogue was once located "near the police station." On-screen, Ashkenazie shows me how he used the mapping tool Wikimapia to find the town's police station and calculate a walking-distance radius around it. Next came diligence plus luck: While scouring Libyan social media, he came across an archival photo that a current Msellata resident happened to post on Facebook, which clearly showed the synagogue across the street from a mosque. Ashkenazie then identified the still-standing mosque from satellite images, thereby confirming the synagogue's former location. "What you don't see are the hours of interviews before we got to the guy who mentioned the police station,"

Ashkenazie says. "It's the work of ants. It's very tedious, but it works."

As I listen to the awe in Ashkenazie's voice, I find myself wondering why anyone would do this "work of ants." Is there really value to documenting this level of detail? At what point does one simply accept that what's past is past? My own great-grandparents, Jewish immigrants from Eastern Europe at the turn of the last century, wanted at all costs to forget the "old country"; this was true for many Middle Eastern Jewish refugees as well, especially those with memories of societies that had turned on them. Ashkenazie admits that many of Diarna's interviewees—mostly elderly Israelis—have to be convinced to sit down with his researchers, baffled as to why anyone would care. The idea that some earnest archivist would call them up and ask them to identify the street corner where their synagogue once stood would have seemed absurd to my ancestors too.

But my cynicism about this "work of ants" quickly slides into a horrifying hopelessness—which is exactly why Diarna's work is so emotionally wrenching to observe. The frightening reality beneath Diarna's efforts is the same one that haunted me as a child. The disappearance of these communities is just an acute (and sometimes violent) version of what eventually happens to every community, everywhere. All of us will die; all of our memories will be lost. Today it's a synagogue in Tunisia that's crumbling; eventually the sun will explode. Why even try?

These questions haunt me as I sift through Diarna's site, along with some unedited video interviews that Ashkenazie

shares with me to give me a sense of the enormous scope
of oral history material Diarna is working to collect, trans-
late, and post: a man describing Yom Kippur in rural Yemen,
a woman detailing the Tomb of Ezra in Iraq, someone else
recalling the Hebrew textbooks he studied in a Cairo school.
The speakers in these videos are deeply foreign to me, elderly
people with Arabic accents describing daily lives I can barely
imagine. Yet they often mention things I recognize: a holiday,
a biblical figure, a prayer, a song. It occurs to me that Jewish
tradition, like every tradition, is designed to protect against
oblivion, capturing ancient experiences in ritual and story and
passing them between generations—and that Diarna is simply
a higher-tech version of what everyone's ancestors once did,
passing along memories around a fire, technology expanding
that warm, bright circle around the fire to the world at large.
I zoom in, listen, as if leaning toward the warmth, the light.
And then, as I click idly from one Diarna file to another, an
invisible curtain rises.

In an oral history video not yet translated or posted online,
an elderly Israeli man speaks in Arabic-accented Hebrew
about his hometown of Yefren in Libya. Up the hill from his
family's branch-ceilinged stone house, he says, was the tiny
town's eight-hundred-year-old synagogue and adjoining ritual
bath. As he sits with a Diarna researcher at his kitchen table in
Israel, he scribbles maps and floorplans, describing the synagogue with its interior arches, its columns, its holy ark for
Torah scrolls. Listening to this man's rambling voice is like
hearing someone recount the elaborate details of a dream—
which is why it is utterly unnerving to click on the town of

Yefren on Diarna's interactive map and find a recent YouTube clip by a British traveler who enters the actual physical ruins of that very synagogue. In the video, the building is a crumbling wreck, but its design is exactly as the Israeli man remembered it. I follow the on-screen tourist in astonishment as he wanders aimlessly through the once-sacred space; I recognize, as if from my own memories, the arches, the columns, the alcove for the Torah scrolls, the water line still visible in the remains of the ritual bath. The "work of ants" actually, magically, works. The effect is humbling, shocking—like seeing a beloved dead relative in a dream. The past is alive, trembling within the present.

The problem is that Diarna's hardworking ants are often digging on a live volcano. This is a region where ISIS and other groups are hell-bent on wiping out minorities, where political upheaval has generated the greatest human migration stream since the end of World War II, and where the deliberate destruction of priceless cultural artifacts sometimes happens because it's Wednesday.

Mapping sites in this environment can require enormous courage—not only because of instability and war, but because the hatred that prompted the Jews' flight has surreally outlived their departure. Libya is one of many places where Jews were violently rejected by their society: Tripoli was more than 25 percent Jewish before World War II, but in 1945 more than a hundred Jews in the city were murdered and hundreds more wounded in massive pogroms, prompting the community's flight. Later, the dictator Muammar Gaddafi expelled all remaining Jews and confiscated their assets. In

2011, after Gaddafi's ouster, a single Libyan Jew who returned and attempted to remove trash from the wreckage of the city's Dar Bishi Synagogue was hounded out of the country by angry mobs waving signs reading NO JEWS IN LIBYA; apparently one was too many.

Earlier that year, a journalist in Tripoli offered to provide Diarna with photos of the once-grand Dar Bishi—a feat requiring Marvel-superhero tactics. "She slipped her minders and broke into the synagogue, which was strewn with garbage, and took pictures of it all," Guberman-Pfeffer told me of the reporter. "Gaddafi's men captured her and confiscated her camera—but the camera was the decoy, and she had pictures on her cell phone." From her photos, Diarna built a 3-D model of the synagogue; the reporter still refuses to be named for fear of repercussions. Other Diarna researchers have resorted to similar subterfuges or narrow escapes. One Kurdish journalist who helped document Iraqi Jewish sites had to flee a poison gas attack.

Even those well beyond war zones often feel on edge. As I spoke with Diarna's devoted researchers—a mix of professionals, student interns, and volunteers—I was alarmed by how many of them warily asked me to let them review any quotes, knowing how haters might pounce on a poorly worded thought. One photographer, who cheerfully told me how he'd gotten access to various Diarna sites by "smiling my way in," suddenly lost his spunk at the end of our conversation as he insisted that I not use his name. If people knew he was Jewish, he confided, he might lose the entrée he needed for his work.

"There's a lot of blood, sweat, and tears to get these images out to the public," says Chrystie Sherman, a photographer who has done multiple expeditions for Diarna—and who took the pictures of the destroyed synagogue in Damascus. Sherman was documenting Tunisian sites for Diarna in 2010 when she decided on her own to go to Syria, despite rumblings of danger. "I was terrified," she remembers. "I left all of my portrait equipment with a friend in Tunis, and just took my Nikon and went to Damascus and prayed to God that I would be OK." Following a lead from a Syrian woman in Brooklyn, she went to the country's last remaining Jewish-owned business, an antique shop in Damascus. The owner took her with other family members to the synagogue, which was no longer used for worship—and where his elderly father, remembering praying there years earlier, sat in his family's old seats and broke down in tears. At another synagogue, Sherman was followed by government agents. "They asked why I was there, and I just told them I was a Buddhist doing a project on different religions. I didn't tell them I was Jewish. You have to think on your feet."

Sherman's photographs for Diarna are incandescent, interiors glowing with color and light. Even her pictures from rural Tunisia, of abandoned synagogues in states of utter ruin, radiate with a kind of warmth, a human witness holding the viewer's hand. "It's hard to describe this feeling, which I have over and over again," she says of her work for Diarna. "You are seeing centuries of Jewish history that have unfolded, and now everything—well, the world has just changed so dramatically and a lot of things are coming to an end." Her words remind me of a Talmudic passage brought to life by the Hebrew poet Chaim Nachman Bialik in an epic work called "Dead of the Desert." The passage and poem describe desert wanderers who discover the mythically preserved bodies of the generation of Israelites—"ageless generation, a people awesome in power, ancient of days"—who died in the desert before reaching the Promised Land, silent witnesses to a forgotten past.

"I was only in Syria for five days, and I was so excited to return with my portrait equipment," Sherman told me. "But then the Arab Spring began, and I couldn't go back."

———

You can't go back. No one ever can. But it's still worth trying.

Because of Diarna, I see my own American landscape differently. I pass by the tiny eighteenth-century cemetery near my home with its Revolutionary War graves, and I think of the histories that might lie unseen alongside the ones we enshrine, wondering whether there might be a Native American burial ground under the local Walgreens, whether I am treading on someone else's ancient sacred space. I know that I must be. We are always walking on the dead.

Yet something more than time's ravages keeps me returning to Diarna. As I explored the photographs and oral histories Diarna has collected, I found myself reeling from yet another antisemitic shooting attack in my own country, this one at a kosher market twenty minutes from my home—its proximity prompting me to hide this information from my children, avoiding mentioning our murdered neighbors. Within days of those murders, my social media feed was already full of pictures from a different attack, at a Los Angeles synagogue where someone—whether hatefully motivated or simply unstable—trashed the sanctuary, dumping Torah scrolls and prayer books on the floor. The pictures reminded me of Sherman's jarring Diarna photos of a ruined synagogue in Tunisia, its floor strewn with holy texts abandoned in piles of dust. Our public spaces today, online and off, are often full of open derision and disrespect for others, of self-serving falsehoods about both past and present, of neighbors turning on neighbors. It's tough these days not to sense an encroaching darkness. Peering through the windows of Diarna's many ruins, I'm looking for more light.

"It's hard to recognize other viewpoints if you're in a bubble where everyone thinks like you," Diarna's research coordinator Ashkenazie tells me. He's talking about homogenized societies in the Middle East, but he could be talking about anywhere, about all of us. "By raising this Jewish history, we're puncturing these bubbles, and saying that in your bubble at one time not long ago, there once were others with you," he says. "It's not so crazy to welcome others."

It's not so crazy. I look through the images of our homes, all of our homes, the windows on my screen wide open.

Chapter 10

BLOCKBUSTER
DEAD
JEWS

THE WEEK I BOUGHT MY ADVANCE TIMED-ENTRY TICKETS
for *Auschwitz: Not Long Ago, Not Far Away,* the massive blockbuster exhibition at the Museum of Jewish Heritage in down-
town Manhattan, there was a swastika drawn on a desk in
my children's public middle school. It was not a big deal. The
school did everything right: It informed parents; teachers
talked to kids; they held an already scheduled assembly with
a Holocaust survivor. Within the next few months, the public
middle school in the adjacent town had six swastikas. That
school also did everything right. Six swastikas were also not
a big deal.

Auschwitz: Not Long Ago, Not Far Away is a big deal. It is
such a big deal that the Museum of Jewish Heritage had to

alter its floor plan to accommodate it, making room for such items as a reconstructed barracks. Outside the museum's front door, there is a cattle car parked on the sidewalk; online, you can watch video footage showing how it was placed there by a crane. The exhibition received massive news coverage, including segments on network TV. When I arrived before the museum opened, the line for ticketholders was already snaking out the door. In front of the cattle car, a jogger was talking loudly on a cell phone about pet sitters.

When I was fifteen years old, I went to the Auschwitz-Birkenau site museum in Poland. I was there with March of the Living, a program that brings thousands of Jewish teenagers from around the world to these sites of destruction. It is the sort of trip that clever people can easily critique. But I was fifteen, and deeply invested in Jewish life, and I found it profoundly moving. Being in these places with thousands of Jewish teenagers felt like a thundering announcement of the Holocaust's failure to eradicate children like me.

That was in the 1990s, when Holocaust museums and exhibitions were opening all over the United States, including the monumental United States Holocaust Memorial Museum in Washington. Going to those new exhibitions then was predictably wrenching, but there was also something hopeful about them. Sponsored almost entirely by Jewish philanthropists and nonprofit groups, these museums were imbued with a kind of optimism, a bedrock assumption that they were, for lack of a better word, effective. The idea was that people would come to these museums and learn what the world had done to the Jews, where hatred can lead. They would then *stop hating Jews*.

It wasn't a ridiculous idea, but it seems to have been proven wrong. A generation later, antisemitism is once again the next big thing, and it is hard to go to these museums today without feeling that something profound has shifted.

––––––––––

In this newest Auschwitz exhibition, something has. *Auschwitz: Not Long Ago, Not Far Away* originated not from Jews trying to underwrite a better future, but from a corporation called Musealia, a for-profit Spanish company whose business is blockbuster museum shows. Musealia's best-known show is the internationally successful *Human Bodies: The Exhibition*, which consisted of cross-sectioned, colorfully dyed cadavers (sourced, it was later revealed, from the Chinese government) that aimed to teach visitors about anatomy and science. Its other wildly popular show is about the *Titanic*. This is, of course, not a disaster-porn company but rather an educational company—and who could argue against education?

Perhaps the earlier Holocaust museums built by the Jewish community were unsuccessful simply because of their limited reach; despite the 2 million annual visitors to the United States Holocaust Memorial Museum, two-thirds of American Millennials in one recent poll were unable to identify what Auschwitz was. Six hundred thousand people saw Musealia's Auschwitz exhibition during its six months in Madrid before it arrived in New York. Those six hundred thousand people have all now heard of Auschwitz. There is apparently a need for more education, despite the efforts of a generation of nonprofit museum educators. As Musealia has demonstrated, there is also public demand.

And the Musealia people clearly know what they are doing. The Auschwitz exhibition was produced in cooperation with numerous museums, most prominently the Auschwitz site museum in Poland, and was carefully curated by diligent historians who are world-renowned experts in this horrific field. It shows.

The Auschwitz exhibition is everything an Auschwitz exhibition should be. It is thorough, professional, tasteful, engaging, comprehensive, clear. It displays more than seven hundred original artifacts from the Auschwitz site museum and collections around the world. It corrects every annoying minor flaw in every other Holocaust exhibition I have ever seen. It does absolutely everything right. And it made me never want to go to another one of these exhibitions ever again.

The exhibition checks all the boxes. There are wall texts and artifacts explaining what Judaism is. Half a room describes premodern antisemitism. There are sections on persecuted Roma, homosexuals, the disabled; the exhibition also carefully notes that 90 percent of those murdered in killing centers like Auschwitz were Jews. There are home movies of Jews before the war, including both religious and secular people. There are video testimonies from survivors.

The exhibition is dependable. There is a room about the First World War's devastation, and another on the rise of Nazism. The audio guide says thoughtful things about bystanders and complicity. There are cartoons and children's picture books showing Jews with hooked noses and bags of money, images familiar today to anyone who has been Jewish on Twitter. There are photos of signs reading KAUFT NICHT BEI JUDEN (Don't buy from Jews), a sentiment familiar today to anyone who has been Jewish on a college campus with a boycott-Israel campaign. There is a section about the refusal of the world to take in Jewish refugees. Somewhere there is a Torah scroll.

The exhibition is relentless. After an hour and a half, I marveled that I was barely past Kristallnacht. *What the hell is taking so long?* I found myself thinking, alarmed by how annoyed I was. *Can't they invade Poland already? Kill us all and get it over with!* It took another hour's worth of audio guide before I made it to the Auschwitz selection ramp, where bewildered Jews were unloaded from cattle cars and separated into those who would die immediately and those who would die in a few more weeks.

Somehow after I got through the gas chambers, there was still, impossibly, another hour left. (*How can there still be an hour left? Isn't everyone dead?*) Slave labor, medical experiments, the processing of stolen goods, acts of resistance, and finally liberation—all of it was covered in what came to feel like a forced march (which, yes, was covered too). It was in the gas-chamber room, where I was introduced to a steel mesh column that, as the wall text explained, was used to drop Zyklon B pesticide pellets into the gas chamber, killing hundreds of naked people within fifteen minutes, that I began to wonder what the purpose of all this is.

I don't mean the purpose of killing millions of people with pesticide pellets in a steel mesh column in a gas chamber. That part, the supposedly mysterious part, is abundantly clear: People will do absolutely anything to blame their problems on others. No, what I'm wondering about is the purpose of my knowing all of these obscene facts, in such granular detail.

I already know the official answer, of course: Everyone must learn the depths to which humanity can sink. Those who do not study history are bound to repeat it. I attended public middle school; I have been taught these things. But as I read the endless wall texts describing the specific quantities of poison used to murder 90 percent of Europe's Jewish children, something else occurred to me. Perhaps presenting all these facts has the opposite effect from what we think. Perhaps we are giving people ideas.

I don't mean giving people ideas about how to murder Jews. There is no shortage of ideas like that, going back to Pharaoh's decree in the Book of Exodus about drowning Hebrew baby boys in the Nile. I mean, rather, that perhaps we are giving people ideas about our standards. Yes, everyone must learn about the Holocaust so as not to repeat it. But this has come to mean that anything short of the Holocaust is, well, not the Holocaust. The bar is rather high.

———

Shooting people in a synagogue in San Diego or Pittsburgh isn't "systemic"; it's an act of a "lone wolf." And it's not the Holocaust. The same is true for arson attacks against two different Boston-area synagogues, followed by similar simultaneous attacks on Jewish institutions in Chicago a few days later, along with physical assaults on religious Jews on the streets of New York—all of which happened within a week of my visit to the Auschwitz show.

Lobbing missiles at sleeping children in Israel's Kiryat Gat, where my husband's cousins spent the week of my museum visit dragging their kids to bomb shelters, isn't an attempt to bring "Death to the Jews," no matter how frequently the people lobbing the missiles broadcast those very words; the wily Jews there figured out how to prevent their children from dying in large piles, so it is clearly no big deal.

Doxxing Jewish journalists is definitely not the Holocaust. Harassing Jewish college students is also not the Holocaust. Trolling Jews on social media is not the Holocaust either, even when it involves photoshopping them into gas chambers. (Give the trolls credit: They have definitely heard of Auschwitz.) Even hounding ancient Jewish communities out of entire countries and seizing all their assets—which happened in a dozen Muslim nations whose Jewish communities predated the Islamic conquest, countries that are now all almost entirely Judenrein—is emphatically not the Holocaust. It is quite amazing how many things are not the Holocaust.

The day of my visit to the museum, the rabbi of my synagogue attended a meeting arranged by police for local clergy, including him and seven Christian ministers and priests. The topic of the meeting was security. Even before the Pittsburgh massacre, membership dues at my synagogue included security fees. But apparently these local churches do not charge their congregants security fees, or avail themselves of government funds for this purpose. The rabbi later told me how he sat in stunned silence as church officials discussed whether to put a lock on a church door. "A *lock on the door*," the rabbi said to me afterward, stupefied.

He didn't have to say what I already knew from the emails the synagogue routinely sends: that they've increased the rent-a-cops' hours, that they've done active-shooter training with the nursery school staff, that further initiatives are in place that "cannot be made public." "A *lock on the door*," he repeated, astounded. "They just have no idea."

He is young, this rabbi—younger than me. He was realizing the same thing I realized at the Auschwitz exhibition, about the specificity of our experience. I feel the need to apologize here, to acknowledge that yes, this rabbi and I both know that many non-Jewish houses of worship in other places also require rent-a-cops, to announce that yes, we both know that other groups have been persecuted too—and this degrading need to recite these middle-school-obvious facts is itself an illustration of the problem, which is that dead Jews are only worth discussing if they are part of something bigger, something more. Some other people might go to Holocaust museums to feel sad, and then to feel proud of themselves for feeling sad. They will have learned something officially important, discovered a fancy metaphor for the limits of Western civilization. The problem is that for us, dead Jews aren't a metaphor, but rather actual people that we do not want our children to become.

The Auschwitz exhibition labors mightily to personalize, to humanize, and these are exactly the moments when its cracks show. Some of the artifacts have stories attached to them, like the inscribed tin engagement ring a woman hid under her tongue. But most of the personal items—a baby carriage, a child's shoe, eyeglasses, a onesie—are completely divorced from the people who owned them. The audio guide humbly speculates about who these people might have been: "She might have been a housewife or a factory worker or a musician . . ." The idea isn't subtle: this woman *could be you*. But to make her you, we have to deny that she was actually herself. These musings turn people into metaphors, and it slowly becomes clear to me that this is the goal. Despite doing absolutely everything right, this exhibition is not that different from *Human Bodies*, full of anonymous dead people pressed into service to *teach us something*.

At the end of the show, on-screen survivors talk in a loop about how people need to love one another. While listening to this, it occurs to me that I have never read survivor literature in Yiddish—the language spoken by 80 percent of victims—suggesting this idea. In Yiddish, speaking only to other Jews, survivors talk about their murdered families, about their destroyed centuries-old communities, about Jewish national independence, about Jewish history, about self-defense, and on rare occasions, about vengeance. Love rarely comes up; why would it? But it comes up here, in this for-profit exhibition. Here it is the ultimate message, the final solution.

That the Holocaust drives home the importance of love is an idea, like the idea that Holocaust education prevents antisemitism, that seems entirely unobjectionable. It is entirely objectionable. The Holocaust didn't happen because of a lack of love. It happened because entire societies abdicated responsibility for their own problems, and instead blamed them on the people who represented—have always represented, since they first introduced the idea of commandedness to the world—the thing they were most afraid of: responsibility.

Then as now, Jews were cast in the role of civilization's nagging mothers, loathed in life, and loved only once they are safely dead. In the years since I walked through Auschwitz at fifteen, I have become a nagging mother. And I find myself furious, being lectured by this exhibition about love—as if the murder of millions of people was actually a morality play, a bumper sticker, a metaphor. I do not want my children to be someone else's metaphor. (Of course, they already are.)

My husband's grandfather once owned a bus company in Poland. Like my husband and some of our children, he was a person who was good at fixing broken things. He would watch professional mechanics repairing his buses, and then never rehired them: he only needed to observe them once, and then he forever knew what to do.

Years after his death, my mother-in-law came across a photograph of her father with people she didn't recognize: a woman and two little girls, about seven and nine years old. Her mother, also a survivor, reluctantly told her that these were her father's original wife and children. When the Nazis came to her father's town, they seized his bus company, and executed his wife and daughters in front of him. Then they kept him alive to repair the buses. They had heard that he was good at fixing broken things.

The Auschwitz exhibition does everything right, and fixes nothing. I walked out of the museum, past the texting joggers by the cattle car, and I felt utterly broken. There is a swastika on a desk in my children's public middle school, and it is no big deal. There is no one alive who can fix me.

Chapter 11

COMMUTING
WITH
SHYLOCK

THIS PLAY TAKES PLACE IN THREE SETTINGS: IN RENAIS-
sance Venice, in Elizabethan England, and in twenty-first-
century New Jersey, in a minivan that smells like gummy
bears. I'll begin with the most important setting, the one with
the gummy bears, because that is the only one that includes a
person I love.

The person I love is my ten-year-old son, though he is not
always an easy person to love. Insistent, demanding, obsessive,
morbid, and often too smart to be pleasant, he needs to get his
way, and for a few recent months I was trapped in the car with
him during a daily commute, forty minutes in each direction.
We survived by listening to podcasts, which I downloaded
by the gigabyte. Fortunately for me, he was fascinated by

Radiolab. Fortunately, that is, until the hosts' banter during an episode about organ ownership devolved into a tangent about a certain famous play, involving a certain famous character who insists and demands, obsessively and morbidly, on receiving default payment on a loan in the form of a pound of flesh.

My son was riveted. "We *need*," he informed me, "to download that play."

I felt slightly ill—both at the prospect of *The Merchant of Venice*, which I had not read in twenty-five years, and at the prospect of yet another showdown with my son. "It's Shakespeare," I tried to deflect. "The language is really hard. I don't think you'll understand it. Besides," I gulped, "*The Merchant of Venice* is—"

"Wait, it's *Shakespeare?*" He had heard of Shakespeare; he was aware that Shakespeare was Important. "If it's Shakespeare, then we totally have to do it! You can always pause it and explain stuff."

I tried to deflect again. "If we're going to read Shakespeare, there are better plays. *Macbeth*, *Hamlet*. This one is—"

"*This one* is about a pound of flesh! I want a pound of flesh!"

He would have his pound of flesh. What happened next is shameful, and the shame is my own.

Late that evening after my children went to sleep, I tooled around online and found a well-reviewed BBC Radio production of *The Merchant of Venice*. Before downloading, I hesitated.

I remembered the visceral feeling of physical nausea I had while reading that play as a student long ago. And I remembered believing the various teachers and professors who assured me and my peers that the play wasn't antisemitic, of course, just a product of its time—and the proof was that it was way better than Christopher Marlowe's *The Jew of Malta*, where the title character expresses his fondness for poisoning wells. After all, didn't Shakespeare make Shylock into a fully realized human, what with his oft-cited eyes, hands, organs, and dimensions? He had eyes, hands, organs, dimensions! If you pricked him, did he not bleed? What greater reassurance did anyone require? In school I accepted all this. Who was I, a teenage girl, to say that Shakespeare was wrong? Unlike teenage girls, who are apparently often mistaken about things like art and sexual assault, Shakespeare was not the sort of person who was wrong.

As I hesitated with my phone in my hand, I had a sudden brainwave. A quarter century had passed since I had read any criticism or scholarship about the play. I had aged, and so had the world. Perhaps Shakespeare was now wrong!

I quickly discovered that Shakespeare was still not wrong. In seconds, I located the enormous volume of scholarly and popular articles published about *The Merchant of Venice* in the years since I first read it. This corpus explained once more, now with an added frisson of wokeness, why the play wasn't antisemitic—not if you really understood it, as vulgar and whiny people often failed to do. It was really a critique of capitalism. It was really a commentary on the Other. It was really a tragedy buried in a comedy. It was really a satire of antisemitism. (Because it's a comedy!) The Christian characters in it were *just as bad*; therefore it was really condemning Christianity. In fact it was a recognition of our common humanity. Shakespeare was the greatest writer who ever lived, and he was simply incapable of creating a character who wasn't fully human.

There were a few outliers in this discussion, like the Yale professor Harold Bloom and the British trial lawyer Anthony Julius. But those who thought the play was irredeemably antisemitic were, the consensus went, vulgar and whiny—and, completely coincidentally, they were also Jewish, which somehow magically invalidated their opinions on this subject. (On the other hand, Jewish scholars who praised the play for its "nuance" were fondly and repeatedly hyperlinked; such pieces, especially in British publications, often advertised the writer's Jewishness with titles like "A Jewish Reading of . . .") A 2016 piece objecting to the play in the *Washington Post* had exclusively negative comments trailing beneath it, most of which said righteous things about "political correctness," "censorship," and "historical context." "What's next," one groused, "getting rid of the Bible?" One comment attacked the article's author, a lawyer with a Jewish surname: "Another power-hungry, mischievous attorney with an axe to grind!" No moderator removed this one-line comment. Like the play, it wasn't antisemitic at all.

Staring into my phone, I sank into my own insecurity, which took the form of a belief that centuries of Shakespearean scholars, and Shakespeare himself, must surely know more than I do. It was a familiar feeling from being a teenage girl, except now it was worse, because now I was feeling it not for myself, but for my son. Wasn't it impressive, after all, that a ten-year-old *wanted* to listen to a play by Shakespeare? How could I, as his parent devoted to educating him, not to mention as an English-language writer myself, shut down my child's earnest desire to share with me his first experience of Shakespeare, the epitome of Western civilization? *Wasn't* Shakespeare the epitome of Western civilization, especially for an English-language writer like me? Wasn't that the whole reason that a ten-year-old wanting to read his work was impressive in the first place?

To my eternal shame, I clicked "Download Now." The next morning in the minivan, we began.

The next scene in this play takes place in Elizabethan England, where a man named William Shakespeare, for supposedly obscure reasons, decided to write a five-act verse comedy—yes, a comedy—whose events unfold largely due to a bloodthirsty Jew.

The reasons are supposedly obscure because Jews were expelled from England in the thirteenth century and were only invited to return in the seventeenth—and thus Shakespeare, the Wikipedia-level thinking goes, is unlikely to ever have met one. But Shakespeare frequently wrote about places he'd never been and types of people he'd never met; Shakespeare's plays appear to be inspired not by personal experiences but by earlier works. This is clearly the case for *The Merchant of Venice*, whose characters and plot are lifted wholesale from a single source, a fourteenth-century Italian story collection called *Il Pecorone* ("The Simpleton") by Giovanni Fiorentino. It's all there in every tiny detail: the young man who falls in love with a rich lady in distant Belmont, the young man's merchant friend who fronts the money for his lovelorn pal's journey, the avaricious Jewish moneylender from whom the merchant gets a loan, the Jew's demand for a pound of flesh in case of default, the trial at which the lady from Belmont disguises herself as a male lawyer, the decree by the "lawyer" that the Jew may take his pound of flesh provided he draw no blood, and even the hijinks involving the woman's ring. The only major difference is that Shakespeare's lady is far nobler than Fiorentino's: in *Merchant*, Portia unhappily fulfills her father's requirements of her suitors, while in *Il Pecorone*, the lady enjoys drugging her suitors and robbing them blind. By removing this detail, Shakespeare removed the suggestion that malicious schemers come from all walks of life. In *Merchant*, there is no such confusion.

It also seems unlikely that Shakespeare was unaware of actual Jews in England, given that one of the biggest news stories in the years immediately preceding the play's composition was the public trial and execution at the Tower of London of a converted Portuguese Jew named Dr. Roderigo Lopez, chief physician to Queen Elizabeth I, who was accused of being paid by the Spanish monarchy to poison the queen. Dr. Lopez, one of the most respected physicians of the sixteenth century, had indiscreetly revealed that he once treated the Earl of Essex for venereal disease. The earl took revenge by framing Dr. Lopez for treason and arranging for his torture; while on the rack, Dr. Lopez "confessed"—though "like a Jew," as the court record states, he denied all charges at trial, while the attorney for the Crown referred to him matter-of-factly as "a perjuring murdering traitor and Jewish doctor."

His execution on Tower Hill in 1594 was accompanied by chants of "Hang the Jew!" from the raucous crowd. But as befitted traitors, Dr. Lopez was not in fact hanged to death, but was rather hanged until partially strangled, and removed from the gallows while still alive. He was then castrated and disemboweled, and his genitalia and intestines were burned before his eyes. After that he was beheaded and pulled by horses into four pieces; these segments of his drawn-and-quartered corpse, along with his severed head, were publicly displayed in separate locations until they decomposed.

It would be vulgar and whiny to overlook the nuances of this situation. After all, the historical record gives Queen Elizabeth a cookie for dawdling on signing Dr. Lopez's death warrant; her doubts about his guilt even led her to mercifully allow his family to keep his property, not unlike the equally merciful Duke of Venice in Shakespeare's play. And it is of course entirely unclear whether this trial and public humiliation of an allegedly greed-driven Jew attempting to murder an upstanding Christian, rapturously reported in the press with myriad antisemitic embellishments, had anything at all to do with Shakespeare's play about the trial and public humiliation of a greed-driven Jew attempting to murder an upstanding Christian—which Shakespeare composed shortly after Dr. Lopez decomposed. Most likely these things were completely unrelated.

———

Our next scene takes place in Renaissance-era Venice, where a fictional man named Antonio needs cash, and borrows some from another fictional man, a character in this Venetian verse play who has a non-Italian name and often speaks in prose. Shylock is certainly a fully human character, what with his speaking in prose and having a non-Italian name, and a familiar human character at that. He is insistent, demanding, obsessive, morbid, too smart to be pleasant, and needs to get his way—or as he puts it, over and over, "I will have my bond."

In reality, Shylock having his bond was never up to him. Whether a person like him would even be permitted to breathe in Renaissance Venice was subject to a charter that had to be renewed every few years; non-renewal was a real possibility, as the Jews discovered during two separate expulsions. In 1516, with Venetian treasuries starved from an expensive war, city authorities looking for new sources of revenue invited Jews—restricted to a few professions including moneylending and running pawnshops—to live in the neighborhood that gave the world the word "ghetto."

The nature of this urban prison, where overcrowding led to "skyscrapers" in which people were stuffed into homes with ceilings under full height, was apparently not well understood by British playwrights. In Shakespeare's play, Shylock's daughter Jessica escapes out her window by night to elope with her Christian lover waiting just below. In the real Venice, Jessica would have had a harder time eloping that evening, considering that the ghetto gates were locked at night and manned by four Christian guards (paid for, as required by Venetian decree, by the Jews themselves), and the ghetto was located on an island whose surrounding canals were guarded all night long by four roving patrol boats to prevent escape (the boat patrols likewise paid for by the Jews). It's possible, of course, that this story is set a bit later, when the ghetto expanded onto the mainland. Accessing the rest of Venice from the mainland part of the ghetto would have required traversing a heavily guarded tunnel under a building—low enough, according to historian Carl Nightingale's history of segregated cities, to force the Jews to bow before the Christian city as they approached it. Outside the ghetto, where Jews were forced to wear yellow badges and hats, one popular public spectacle was the burning of the Talmud, all copies of which were confiscated and torched by 1553.

Such precautions were necessary because of the enormous threat. The consequences of allowing Jews to live in one's city were vividly illustrated in 1475 in the Italian town of Trent, about 130 miles from Venice, where the entire Jewish population was subjected to elaborate tortures until they "confessed" to murdering a Christian toddler named Simon in order to eat his flesh and blood. For everyone's safety, Jews were burned alive and their assets confiscated, while Simon was canonized as a saint.

This incident occurred just in time for word to spread via high-tech new media, which could disseminate lies at an unprecedented pace. Many of Italy's very first printed books were about Jews butchering and eating this child, with lurid illustrations that today would qualify as deep fakes. These cartoons and their accompanying texts inspired the planting of children's corpses in Jewish homes and the subsequent public executions of Jews in at least five other Italian towns within ten years. Venice's government, eager to maintain its Jewish tax base, officially discouraged the blood libel, but the population was more inspired by the renowned Venetian poet laureate Raffaele Zovenzoni—whose hymn describing the sainted child's murder, which begged authorities to protect the people from bloodthirsty Jews, went viral. Within a few generations, Venice's brilliant idea of imprisoning Jews in ghettos went viral too.

———————

Our final scene unfolds in twenty-first century New Jersey, in the minivan fragrant with gummy bears, where I decided to prepare my son for what he was about to hear.

"There's something you need to know about this play," I told him as we pulled out of the driveway. "The guy who wants the pound of flesh is Jewish. And the way this play shows this guy is . . . well, it's what we call antisemitic."

"Ooh, vocab word!" my son yelped. *Vocab word*, I thought, and tried to cheer myself up. *See, we're learning here! Learning is good!* "What's that?"

"It means people who hate Jews."

At ten, my son was familiar with this concept. "Like in the Passover story, or the Purim story, or the Hanukkah story? Or like that guy who shot people in Pittsburgh?"

"Yeah. Like that." I grimaced, thinking of the shootings, beatings, and stabbings since then, the ones I made a point of not telling him about. "Only in this play, it's not about killing people. It's about making Jews into a mean cartoon of a bad guy." It occurred to me, as I gripped the steering wheel, that these two things were in fact not at all separate, that the cartoon brand of hatred was actually the prerequisite for the killing-people brand of hatred, from Simon of Trent to Pepe the Frog. I chose not to explain this. Later it occurred to me that my failure to explain this, my perpetuation of the lie that the trolling was distinct from the danger, was part of the problem. My son did not notice.

"So that's why there's the weird stuff about a pound of flesh?" he asked.

"Exactly," I said. Then my loyalty to the glories of Western civilization kicked in, and I felt the need to add: "This play does cartoony stuff with this character, but Shakespeare also makes the guy more real. He isn't just a greedy bad guy; it's more complicated than that. He's human too."

My son was getting antsy. He would have his bond. "Play it," he demanded. I did.

The BBC production was vivid and engrossing. To my surprise I only needed to pause the playback occasionally to explain sixteenth-century puns, along with the concept of "usury," which baffled my son: "Don't people need to be able to borrow money to buy houses and stuff? Why is that bad?" I had no answer for this. But with the entrance of Shylock, there was far more to explain.

Shylock enters with the words "Three thousand ducats," and then says of the noble Antonio, "I hate him for he is a Christian; / But more for that in low simplicity / He lends out money gratis and brings down / The rate of usuance here with us in Venice. / If I can catch him once upon the hip, / I will feed fat the ancient grudge I bear him."

"Pause it," my son demanded from the backseat. "What does that mean?"

"Um, which part?" I asked, stalling. There was no good part.

"The part about why he hates the guy. He hates him for being Christian? That's dumb. But what's his other reason?" he asked, clearly hoping the other reason was a better one.

It wasn't a better one. "Because Shylock wants more money," I said.

"I thought you said he's not just a greedy bad guy."

"He's not," I claimed. "It gets better."

It did not get better. Soon I was forced to explain Shylock's self-serving interpretation of the biblical Jacob (a story my son knew in a sacred context), Antonio's fondness for spitting on Shylock, Shylock's deal for the pound of flesh, and numerous other verses that were painful to elucidate for one's Jewish ten-year-old son, such as "The Hebrew will turn Christian; he grows kind."

I drove in a daze, stunned by the sheer awfulness of it, dreading every verse my son would ask me to explain. The quality of mercy is not strain'd, the play's heroine famously says, but I strained to recall all the merciful interpretations of the play's richness, its "nuance." It was damned hard to hear the nuance while parsing lines like "Certainly the Jew is the very devil incarnal," or "My master's a very Jew; give him a present, give him a halter," or explaining what Shylock meant when he planned to "go in hate, to feed upon / The prodigal Christian." About an hour in—after Shylock's daughter escaped her evil father ("Our house is hell"), but before Shylock declared that he'd rather his daughter be "dead at my foot . . . and the ducats in her coffin"—we made it to Shylock's famous monologue, the part that makes it all OK.

I hit Pause, knowing I needed to build this up. "This speech changes what you think of Shylock," I told my son. "It makes him more human."

My son put on his game face. "OK, let's hear it."

The actor began the brief soliloquy that every English-speaking Jew is apparently meant to take as a compliment: "I am a Jew. Hath not a Jew eyes? Hath not a Jew hands, organs, dimensions, senses, affections, passions? . . . If you prick us, do we not bleed? If you tickle us, do we not laugh? If you poison us, do we not die? And if you wrong us, shall we not revenge?"

"Wait, *that's* the part where he's more human?"

I hit Pause again. "Sure," I told my son, game-facing him back in the rearview. "He's reminding us how he's like everyone else. He's a normal person with normal feelings."

My son laughed. "You seriously fell for that?"

I swallowed, sickened. "What do you mean?"

"Shylock's just saying he wants revenge! Like, 'Oh, yeah? If I'm a regular human, then I get to be *eee-vil* like a regular human!' This is the evil monologue thing that every supervillain does! 'I've had a rough life, and if you were me you would do the same thing, so that's why I'm going to KILL BATMAN, mu-hahaha!' He's just manipulating the other guy even more!"

"No, he's—" I fumbled, remembering the monologue's final words: *The villainy you teach me, I will execute; / and it shall go hard but I will better the instruction.* For the first time I heard the unspoken phrase that followed it: *Mu-hahaha.* I'd been trolled, betrayed, like Shylock at court.

"You're not supposed to *fall for* the evil supervillain monologue! What idiot would fall for that?"

What idiot would? I would. I did. I stared at the road in shame. My son is insistent, demanding, obsessive, morbid, too smart to be pleasant. It had not previously occurred to me that those traits are also his greatest strengths, the sources of his integrity.

"That was pathetic," he muttered. It was unclear whether he was referring to the play, or to his mother. "Are there other parts where he actually acts normal? Or is that it?"

Was that it? I reviewed the other moments scholars cite to prove Shylock's "humanity." There were two lines of Shylock treasuring his dead wife's ring, unlike the play's Christian men who give their wives' rings away. But unlike the other men, Shylock never gets his ring back—because his daughter steals it, and becomes a Christian, and inherits what remains of his estate at the play's triumphant end. Then there was the trial scene, where modern actors often make Shylock seem tragic rather than horrific. But that was performance, not text. Finally, scholars point to the many times Shylock *explains* why he is so revolting: Christians treat him poorly, so he returns the favor. But for this to satisfy, one must accept that Jews are revolting to begin with, and that their repulsiveness simply needs to be explained. None of it worked. And then I saw just how deep the gaslighting went: *I* felt obligated to make it work, to contort this revolting material into something that excused it.

I have a doctorate in literature. I am aware that Shakespeare's plays contain many layers and mean many things. But the degrading hideousness of this character is obvious even to a ten-year-old, and no matter how many more layers the play contains, that is unambiguously one of them. Why, I wondered, should I feel obligated to excuse this blindingly obvious fact, like some abused wife explaining why her darling husband beat her up? Why did I need to participate in this perverse historical mind trick of justifying my own people's humiliation—a humiliation that was never just a cartoon but that cost so many of my ancestors their dignity and even their lives?

"Nope," I told my son. "That's it."

"That's *it*?! That totally sucked."

"It gets worse," I said. How could I have exposed my child to this? "Let's turn it off."

But my son is insistent, demanding, obsessive, morbid. When you prick him, he does not bleed. "I need to hear how it ends."

The trial scene was agonizing. We listened together as Shylock went to court to extract his pound of flesh; as the heroine, chirping about the quality of mercy, forbade him to spill the Christian's blood as he so desperately desired; as the court confiscated his property, along with his soul through forced conversion; as the play's most cherished characters used his own words to taunt and demean him, relishing their vanquishing of the bloodthirsty Jew. My son stopped asking me to explain. Twenty minutes of congratulatory hijinks followed Shylock's final exit, as the cast reveled in their victory and his seized assets. At last it was over.

The minivan fell silent. Then my son announced, "I never want to hear that again."

"You will definitely hear that again," I said.

It's true. "Censorship" is beside the point, the insane extremes of "cancel culture" extravagantly irrelevant, because this double helix of hate and art is built into our world. My son will read this play in school. Or he will hear about a new performance; it's one of the most performed plays Shakespeare ever wrote. He will encounter headlines and jokes using the phrase "pound of flesh." He couldn't even make it through a season of *Radiolab* without it. There is a terrible bond at work here, tying us inexorably to a long history of ugly caricatures and spilled blood. And there is also a much subtler and more insidious bond, tying us to the need to justify and accept it. But unlike me, my son insists on integrity, demands it. He is not afraid to be unpleasant; he knows evil when he hears it. He is ready for this bond.

I told him, "At least now you know."

"Yes," he said, and smiled. "Next can we download *Dracula*?"

Chapter 12

DEAD AMERICAN JEWS, PART THREE:

Turning the Page

THE THIRD TIME THERE WAS A SHOOTING ATTACK AGAINST American Jews, the *New York Times* did not call me to ask for a quick op-ed, and neither did anyone else. I presume this was because when something happens three times, it is no longer news. Perhaps these news outlets realized just how unnewsworthy this story actually was. People murdering Jews, as a three-thousand-year-old global phenomenon, is pretty much the opposite of news. When no one called me, I felt profoundly relieved, because the things I wanted to say about it were no longer things that I could actually say.

The third shooting attack, and the dozen or so other physical attacks on American Jews that followed in rapid succession after it—some barely reported—were what privately changed me, perhaps because that third shooting happened at a kosher grocery store about twenty minutes from my house.

Unlike after the Pittsburgh and San Diego attacks, information on the Jersey City attack was slow to accumulate. The two assailants first killed a livery driver (it was later discovered that they had Googled his Jewish-sounding surname), then progressed to killing a police officer who had noticed their stolen U-Haul, and then proceeded to attack the grocery store, resulting in a protracted gun battle in which the grocery's owner, a customer, and a store worker were killed, along with the two assailants, who were killed by police after an exchange of fire that lasted well over an hour. The scene in the city was dramatic: Entire neighborhoods swarmed with state troopers and the National Guard, and children in nearby schools were held in lockdowns until late at night.

The event was initially reported as a kind of perp chase gone horribly wrong, during which criminals outrunning cops ducked into a random store for cover. But antisemitic screeds found in the attackers' vehicle and in their social media postings told a different story, as did the tactical gear they wore, the massive stash of ammunition and firearms they brought along, and security camera footage showing them driving slowly down the street, checking addresses before parking and entering the market with guns blazing. Then there were the enormous quantities of explosives in their stolen truck, which an FBI agent later said had the capacity to kill people within a range of five hundred yards. Their real targets, authorities surmised, were likely the fifty Jewish children in the private elementary school at the same address, directly above the store—all of whom huddled in closets for the entire gun battle, listening to their neighbors being murdered below.

The delayed clarity on what exactly happened in Jersey City muted some of the public empathy that instantly followed the previous attacks. So did the identities of the attackers, both of whom were Black, and their targets, who were Hasidic Jews—who, it has progressively become clear, many otherwise enlightened Americans view as absolutely fair game for bigotry.

This was obvious from reporting within hours of the attack, which gave surprising emphasis to the murdered Jews as "gentrifying" a "minority" neighborhood. This was remarkable, given that the tiny Hasidic community in question, highly visible members of the world's most consistently persecuted minority, in fact came to Jersey City *fleeing* gentrification, after being priced out of long-established Hasidic communities in Brooklyn. More tellingly, as the journalist Armin Rosen has pointed out, the apparently murderous rage against gentrification has yet to result in anyone using automatic weapons to blow away white hipsters at the newest Blue Bottle Coffee franchise. What was most remarkable about this angle, however, was how it was presented in media reports as providing "context."

The "context" supplied by news outlets after this attack was breathtaking in its cruelty. As the Associated Press explained in a news report about the Jersey City murders that was picked up by NBC and many other outlets, "The slayings happened in a neighborhood where Hasidic families had recently been relocating, amid pushback from some local officials who complained about representatives of the community going door to door, offering to buy homes at Brooklyn prices." (Like many homeowners, I too have been approached by real estate agents asking me if I wanted to sell my home. I recall saying no, though I suppose murdering these people would also have made them go away.) New Jersey's state newspaper, the *Star-Ledger*, helpfully pointed out that "the attack that killed two Orthodox Jews, an Ecuadorian immigrant and a Jersey City police detective has highlighted racial tension that had been simmering ever since ultra-Orthodox Jews began moving to a lower-income community"—even though the assailants never lived in Jersey City, and apparently chose their target simply through internet searches for Jewish institutions in the New York area. The *Washington Post* began its analysis of the murders by announcing that Jersey City "is grappling with whether the attack reflects underlying ethnic tensions locally and fears that it could spark new ones"—even though the rest of the article described in detail how "longtime black residents and ultra-Orthodox implants alike say that they haven't experienced significant ethnic tensions here." Nonetheless, readers were informed, "the influx of Hasidic residents comes as many of the longtime black residents feel increasingly squeezed." This was all about gentrification, the public learned. The assailants, who wore socially acceptable clothing, were expressing an understandable communal sentiment. The newly dead Jews, on the other hand, were members of the unharassed majority, despite being the country's top hate-crime target according to the FBI. They were also rich, despite experiencing the same poverty rates as the rest of New York and New Jersey. On top of that, they wore unfashionable hats. So it kind of made sense that people wanted to murder their children with high-impact explosives.

I was not able to find any similar "context" in media reports after the 2015 massacre at a Black church in Charleston, South Carolina, or the 2016 massacre at an LGBTQ nightclub in Orlando, Florida, or the 2019 massacre at a Walmart in El Paso, Texas frequented by Latino shoppers— all hate-crime attacks that unambiguously targeted minority groups. In each of those cases, as was true in Jersey City, media coverage included sympathetic pieces about the victims, along with investigative pieces about the perpetrators, the latter focused on how perpetrators were drawn into violent irrational hatred. But in reviewing media reports from the aftermath of these events, I found no coverage of how straight people in Orlando other than the perpetrator—in other words, reasonable, non-murderous, relatable "normal" neighbors—were understandably upset about gay couples setting up shop in the neighborhood and disrupting their "way of life," or about how white people with deep family roots in Charleston felt understandably wistful about the Black community's "takeover" of certain previously white neighborhoods, or about how non-Latinos in El Paso felt "squeezed" by ongoing "tensions" with Latinos who had pushed for more bilingualism in schools.

No one covered this "context," because doing that would be bonkers. It would be hateful victim-blaming, the equivalent of analyzing the flattering selfies of a rape victim in lurid detail in order to provide "context" for a sexual assault.

That doesn't mean that intergroup tensions (or the problems with flattering selfies) aren't ever worth examining. It simply means that presenting such analysis as a hot take after a massacre is not merely disgusting and inhuman, but also a form of the very same hatred that caused the massacre—because the sole motivation for providing such "context" in that moment is to inform the public that those people got what was coming to them. People who think of themselves as educated and ethical don't do this, because it is both factually untrue and morally wrong. But if we're talking about Hasidic Jews, it is quite literally a different story, and there is one very simple reason why.

The mental gymnastics required to get the Jersey City attack out of my head were challenging, especially when the Jewish community in the New York area was treated in the two weeks following this massacre to more than a dozen other assaults of varying degrees, most of them coming during the festival of Hanukkah. These included Jews being slapped, punched, kicked, and beaten on the streets by people who made their motives clear by shouting antisemitic insults, and many other variants on this theme that received much less attention. (One that shook me personally was when a young white man broke into my students' dormitory at Yeshiva University at four a.m. and started a fire—using matches from the dorm lobby's Hanukkah candle-lighting.) All this was merely an intensified version of physical assaults on Hasidic Jews in New York that had been happening regularly for over a year—incidents that ranged from run-of-the-mill acts of knocking elderly people to the ground to the rather more advanced tactic of clobbering someone over the head with a large paving stone, causing a fractured skull.

This new normal culminated in a particularly horrifying attack, when a man entered a crowded Hanukkah party at a Hasidic rabbi's house in Monsey, New York, wielding a four-foot machete, and stabbed or slashed five people, all of whom were hospitalized; one victim, who fell into a coma, died several months later from his wounds. Stabbing Jews was apparently in vogue in Monsey, as this was actually the second antisemitic knifing in town in just over a month. The previous attack's victim was beaten and stabbed while walking to morning prayers, winding up in critical condition with head injuries. Media coverage of these attacks also sometimes featured "context" (read: gaslighting), mentioning heated schoolboard or zoning battles between Hasidic and non-Hasidic residents—even after the perpetrator was identified as a resident of a town forty minutes away. One widely syndicated *Associated Press* article situated the previous week's bloodbath by informing millions of readers that "The expansion of Hasidic communities in New York's Hudson Valley, the Catskills and northern New Jersey has led to predictable sparring over new housing development and local political control. It has also led to flare-ups of rhetoric seen by some as antisemitic." In other words, the cause of bloodthirsty antisemitic violence is . . . Jews, living in a place! Sometimes, Jews who live in places even *buy land on which to live.* To be fair, there were many countries and centuries in which this Jews-owning-land monkey business was illegal, though twenty-first-century Hudson Valley, the Catskills, and northern New Jersey are sadly not among those enlightened locales. Predictably, this leads to sparring, and flare-ups. Who *wouldn't* express frustration with municipal politics by hacking people with a machete?

After the first attack in Pittsburgh, I was devastated. After the second attack in San Diego, I was angry. But after the third attack near my home and the season of horror that followed, I simply gave up.

There was no way I could write about any of this for the *New York Times*, or any other mainstream news outlet. I could not stomach all the "to be sures" and other verbal garbage I would have to shovel in order to express something acceptable to a non-Jewish audience in a thousand words or less. I could no longer handle the degrading exercise of calmly explaining to the public why it was not OK to partially amputate someone's arm with a four-foot-long blade at a holiday party, even if one had legitimate grievances with that person's town council votes. Nor could I announce, as every non-Jewish media outlet would expect, that these people whose hairstyles one dislikes are "canaries in the coal mine," people whose fractured skulls we all ought to care about because they *serve as a warning*—because when Jews get murdered or maimed, it might be an ominous sign that *actual* people, people who wear athleisure, might *later* get attacked! I was done with this sort of thing, which amounted to politely persuading people of one's right to exist.

The thought of writing about any of this for Jewish media outlets was sickening for a different reason. It was demoralizing to confront the American Jewish community's ongoing and escalating panic, the completely justified intergenerational PTSD freak-out voiced constantly from every point on the political spectrum, the repetitive anxiety attacks expressed on social media, the nonstop discussion about whether this was like Berlin in 1935. This facile comparison was of course ridiculous on its face, as well as insulting to the overwhelming majority of Americans who responded to these attacks in exactly the opposite fashion from the mass state-sponsored violence of Nazi Germany. If anything, this felt more like Paris in 2005—a place where there was no shortage of legal protections and official goodwill, but where one wouldn't be crazy to occasionally hide a yarmulke under a baseball hat. Yet the thought of explaining this was exhausting too, and also beside the point. Was I really going to expend energy delineating why this wasn't like the Third Reich, but perhaps resembled, say, second-century Egypt or tenth-century Spain? To what end? To reassure everyone that "only" a few Jews were actually maimed or dead, so everything was cool? Nitpicking over sloppy historical analogies was a convenient distraction. The fact was that a communal memory of multiple millennia had been activated, and it was deep and real.

Of all the tedious and self-serving explanations for why this scourge was apparently reemerging in American life (*Guns! Trump! Trolls! Twitter!*), the most convincing was actually the most boring, and also the most disturbing: The last few generations of American non-Jews had been chagrined by the enormity of the Holocaust—which had been perpetrated by America's enemy, and which was grotesque enough to make antisemitism socially unacceptable, even shameful. Now that people who remembered the shock of those events were dying off, the public shame associated with expressing antisemitism was dying too. In other words, hating Jews was normal. And historically speaking, the decades in which my parents and I had grown up simply hadn't been normal. Now, normal was coming back.

A week after that horrific Hanukkah, the Jewish community organized a "No Fear, No Hate" march in New York City, which twenty-five thousand people attended—though almost no one from the particular Hasidic communities which had been attacked, whose adherents generally don't go in for that sort of thing. I didn't go in for it either, though for somewhat different reasons. It interfered with Hebrew school carpooling, for one thing. And while I knew the march was intended as an act of pride and defiance and that those who attended found it empowering and inspiring, its mere existence felt profoundly depressing to me, almost like an admission of defeat. I watched the photos and videos pouring in from the march with a kind of uncomfortable schadenfreude: happy that so many people had attended, and even happier that I was obligated to drive seven children home from Hebrew school instead.

But another massive Jewish gathering near my home a few days earlier had also caught my attention, one whose attendance, ninety thousand people at MetLife Stadium in New Jersey's Meadowlands, dwarfed that of the march in New York. And unlike the march, it was attended by many of the people who had been directly targeted during those horrific weeks. This event, which was mirrored in parallel events around the world, was the "Siyum HaShas," or "Conclusion of the Talmud," a ceremony celebrating the completion of communally studying the Babylonian Talmud in a program called Daf Yomi, or "A Page a Day."

Begun by a Polish rabbi in 1923 as a way to democratize Talmud study, the premise of Daf Yomi is to study one "page" of the Talmud each day—really two sides of one large physical page, which with the necessary commentaries is more like fifteen pages of dense material—thereby completing the Talmud's 2,711 "pages" in a very reasonable seven and a half years. To those unfamiliar with Jewish text study, this probably sounds like a big commitment. But when one considers that Talmud study was traditionally a full-time affair, it was quite radical to suggest that one could actually complete the entire Talmud while still, say, holding down a job. Today, Daf Yomi, the "world's largest book club," consists of hundreds of thousands of people around the world who spend those seven and a half years quite literally on the same page. When they finish, most of them start right over again.

I wouldn't have fit in much at MetLife Stadium's Daf Yomi ceremony, which consisted almost entirely of men wearing black hats. Since the fifth century when the Talmud was compiled (its sources span the previous six centuries), women have rarely studied it. Its study was also long deemphasized in Judaism's more liberal modern movements, including those in which I was raised. But in recent years, both of those things have been changing. This most recent Daf Yomi cycle concluded with a large-scale women's ceremony in Jerusalem, attended by thousands of women—many of whom had not only studied the text for the previous seven and a half years, but had also taught it, sometimes for large audiences in person and online. My brilliant friend Ilana Kurshan, an accomplished literary agent and translator in Jerusalem, published an award-winning memoir, *If All the Seas Were Ink*, describing how the daily routine of Talmud study carried her through challenging years in her own life—and her book inspired many less-traditional people who had previously assumed that Talmud study wasn't for them. In the years since the last cycle began, Daf Yomi resources had also blossomed online, including a fantastic variety of podcasts, Facebook discussion groups, Instagram stories, Twitter accounts, and more, much of it geared toward people with no previous background in Talmud study. Daf Yomi was going viral.

I had toyed with doing Daf Yomi at the start of the last cycle, but I had just given birth to my fourth baby, and the thought of slogging through fat volumes or clunky websites with mediocre translations was unappealing at best. But this time around, there was a game-changing free app called Sefaria (Hebrew for "library"), which contained nearly the entire canon of traditional Jewish texts in their original Hebrew and Aramaic, along with more accessible English translations. I'd downloaded Sefaria years earlier—it was created by an acquaintance—and I often relied on it for biblical and other references. On that frigid and depressing Sunday in January, toggling on my phone between the vast crowds of anti-hate marchers and the vast crowds of Talmud enthusiasts, I realized with utter wonder that I already had the entire Talmud in the palm of my hand.

I suddenly knew what I wanted to do. Along with hundreds of thousands of people around the world, I opened to the very first page, and began.

———

Something magical happened when I switched over from looking online at news reports about antisemitic attacks to joining online Daf Yomi discussion groups and looking up Daf Yomi resources. The algorithms all caught on instantly, and suddenly I saw almost nothing online that wasn't related to discussions of the Talmud's opening pages—which contain a rambling, digressive, and almost bottomless conversation about when, where, and how to recite the Sh'ma, Judaism's central statement of faith in the singularity of God.

I had studied parts of the Talmud before, and in the past I'd found its structure extraordinarily annoying. The Talmud isn't written like a normal book, or even like a normal "sacred" text. It's not a story, or a manual of religious practice, or a compilation of wisdom, or a book of philosophy, or a commentary on the Bible, or even a compendium of laws. Instead, it's more like a ridiculously long social media thread, complete with pedantic back-and-forths, hashtagged references, nonstop links and memes, and limitless subthreads, often with almost no discernible arc or goal. Or to use a more timeless metaphor, it's like walking into a room full of people engaged in a heated conversation—people who are constantly interrupting one another and shunting the conversation onto different tracks, and who don't care at all if you know what they're talking about, and who therefore never bother to explain why any of this matters. For a novelist like me who spent twenty years creating artistically designed stories, engineered to draw readers in and take them to a destination, this rambling discussion passing itself off as a book (recorded, incidentally, in a nearly indecipherable shorthand style) always struck me as exasperating in the extreme. But after the dark weeks I had just sleepwalked through and all the inexpressible anxiety that had accompanied them, I walked into this irritating conversation and experienced a strange and unexpected feeling: an undeniable sense of welcome and relief. It was like coming out of a cold, dark night into a warm and lighted room. Six centuries of sages seemed to move over, still talking, and make space for me at the study-hall table strewn with open books. I sat down, exhausted, and listened.

————

From when, the Talmud's first page begins, does one recite the evening Sh'ma? From when the priests in the Temple consumed the daily sacrifices. From when the remains of those sacrifices finished burning on the altar. From dusk, which is different from sunset. Up until midnight. Actually, up until dawn. How do you know when it's dawn? When you can distinguish between a white and a blue thread, the threads sewn into the corner of a garment to remind one of God's commandments—but they'll get back to that later. Really it's up to the end of the first night watch. Or the second watch. How long is a "watch," and how many are there in the night? A biblical verse suggests there are four. Another verse suggests there are three. During the first night watch, donkeys bray; during the second night watch, dogs bark; during the third, babies wake to nurse and wives whisper with their husbands. Maybe this is beautiful imagery, or maybe it corresponds to constellations moving across the night sky. This whole conversation is about how to tell time without clocks—or, to put it another way, how to find one's place in the world while the world is in motion, how to hold fast to that constant point of stillness as all else changes. It's a skill, a science, an art. King David woke at midnight to praise God, according to the Psalms. How did he wake up? He had an Aeolian harp hanging above his bed, and the midnight wind would wake him. Would the wind always come at midnight? Or was this wind more like a writer's inspiration, moving the poet-king to rise in the dark and write his psalms of praise?

It had been a number of years since I had regularly recited the evening Sh'ma. But after spending half an hour each day following complex arguments on this point, I found myself returning to it, on my own and with my family, chanting the words as we drifted to sleep. There was a comfort here, a refuge as we recited the words. We were on a watch, awake in the dark. But someone was also watching us.

There was also something comforting in the endlessness of the rabbis' conversations. The obsessive-compulsive thought patterns of these people felt familiar to me, a personality tic that I knew well from myself and from many of my relatives and friends—one that had always frustrated me, both in myself and in others. I'd perceived it as a fault to be corrected. But now I saw clearly what it was expressing: grief, fear, and resilience.

Until the year 70 CE, Judaism had been centered at the ancient Temple in Jerusalem, where worship was mediated through priests offering sacrifices. This was a visceral, physical process involving livestock and grain and wine and incense and fire and smoke. There was nothing metaphorical or intellectual about it. Even the location itself was mandated by God. After the Romans destroyed this temple and exiled the people, there was no particular reason for this religion, or even simply this people, to survive in any form. But on the eve of this temple's destruction, one sage, Rabbi Yochanan ben Zakkai, had himself smuggled out of the besieged city of Jerusalem in a coffin, after which he convinced the Roman general Vespasian to allow him to open an academy for Torah scholars in a small town far from Jerusalem. Both Rabbi Yochanan ben Zakkai and Judaism faked their own deaths in order to survive this cataclysm. The small cadre of scholars in that small town reinvented this religion by turning it into a virtual-reality system, replacing temple rituals with equally ritualized blessings and prayers, study of Torah, and elaborately regulated interpersonal ethics. The sages frantically arguing about when and how to recite which prayers are survivors and descendants of survivors, remnants of a destroyed world. They are anxious about remembering every last detail of that lost connection to God, like mourners obsessing over the tiniest memories of a beloved they have lost. One might expect that this memory would eventually fade, that people would "move on." Instead the opposite happens. Once the process of memory becomes important, the details do not fade but rather accrue—because the memory itself becomes a living thing, enriched by every subsequent generation that brings new meaning to it.

As I followed the discussions that had previously annoyed

me, I realized something stunning: Many of the sages arguing with one another on each page didn't live in the same generation, or even in the same century. Nor were they, for the most part, quoting written texts of what those in the previous generation or century had said. Instead, they relied on designated people who served as mental court reporters, tasked with sitting in study halls where these discussions took place and mentally recording entire conversations between sages. These records were then passed down almost entirely orally, written down only generations later.

This would simply be a fascinating historical fact, except that as I turned the Talmud's pages, I discovered that it wasn't—because these people's elaborate communal memory overlapped with mine. As I followed along while the rabbis debated how prayers should be said, I frequently bumped up against actual prayers and practices—blessings of gratitude for different foods, words to recite before a journey, how and when to bow and rise—that I myself had learned when I was young, that I too knew by heart. Of course, I only knew these things because of these people on this page, and all the people after them, who had made the conscious decision to pass these things down to me. None of these sages needed to say what was obvious from the mere existence of this process. Destruction and humiliation didn't matter. Only memory and integrity did. Was the hour I was living through right now different from the hour they were living through then? Did it matter? From what hour does one recite the evening Sh'ma?

God prays, the sages say. There is a lot on God's mind. According to the Psalms, God is furious every day. How long does God remain angry? the sages ask. For one fifty-eight thousand eight hundred and eighty-eighth of an hour. In God's prayer, God says: *May it be my will that my compassion will overcome my anger.* I wondered: Was I furious every day too? (I was, then.) Could I try to be furious only for one fifty-eight thousand eight hundred and eighty-eighth of an hour? Could my compassion overcome my anger? Was my life a mere fifty-eight thousand eight hundred and eighty-eighth of an hour? From what hour does one recite the evening Sh'ma?

I was surprised by how little I was bothered by the things I didn't agree with. Perhaps you will be shocked to hear, for instance, that a fifth-century text says unenlightened things about women. I could hardly have cared less. I was more surprised by how enchanted I was by what almost no one would agree with, or at least no mature adult.

The Torah wasn't given to the ministering angels, one sage points out, but to people with bodies. Bodies that fart. There is an entirely unreasonable amount of material about bathrooms, farting, peeing, and pooping, which is off-putting if you are not a twelve-year-old boy. Luckily I live with a twelve-year-old boy, along with a ten-year-old boy and a seven-year-old boy—and boy, were they entertained. This opened my eyes to how much of the text was perhaps intentionally funny. One extended discussion, for instance, dealt with whether one could recite the Sh'ma while in the presence of a pile of poop. Walk at least four steps away from it, one sage advised. But what if you still smell it? another asked. Well, another chimed in, perhaps it depended whether the poop was wet or dry. But how can you determine *how* dry the poop is? somebody asked—and then promptly supplied a story of how one revered teacher once sent his devoted pupil to check the specific crustiness of a piece of poop. My sons' amusement at this made me realize what should have been obvious: The discussion might have been serious (especially before indoor plumbing), but there might well be a point where it crossed over to deadpan humor. Or bedpan humor. Either way, then as now, the world really is full of shit. We can pretend the shit is not there, or we can think through how to live with it without making ourselves sick.

Similar trolling powers arose in a discussion of invisible "demons" that, various sages claimed, surrounded each person by the thousands, causing all kinds of pains and illnesses. (Two major twentieth-century sages suggested a new translation for the ambiguous word "demons": germs.) Was there a way to see these "demons"? the sages wondered. Yes, one rabbi announced. One simply had to take the placenta of a firstborn black cat, who was herself the firstborn daughter of another firstborn black cat, grind up and burn that cat placenta, and then rub it into one's eyes—"and then one will see them." Another sage followed these instructions and saw the demons, which probably looked like ground-up burnt cat placenta. I could not stop laughing. On the other hand, demons really are everywhere. They are invisible, and there are thousands of them, on every screen in every pocket, spreading lies and causing pain. God is furious every day. Who isn't?

The sages mourn. One rabbi, father of ten dead sons, carries around a bone of his tenth dead son and shows it to every mourner he meets, sharing his pain and also his compassion.

Another, asked to serenade a bride and groom, stands and sings, *You are going to die.* Others smash glasses at weddings, a practice continued at my own. Ours is a broken world. Rebuilding is hard, daily, constant, endless, the marriage that follows the wedding, which is not a happy ending but an imperfect beginning. From when can we recite the evening Sh'ma?

The sages obsess over how to disagree without humiliating others. One announces that it is preferable to enter a fiery furnace than to embarrass another person in public. When the president of the rabbinic high court publicly insults a sage who disagrees with him, the court impeaches him and throws him out of office. Seeing the respect given to the sage he insulted, the former president visits him at home, where he discovers the sage is a humble blacksmith. He begs forgiveness, repeating his apologies even when the man at first ignores him. When the man accepts his apology, the court restores him to his position, though on the condition that he share the post with the sage appointed in his stead—a compromise reached with the help of the blacksmith sage, on behalf of his former enemy. I studied these passages as the news blared with a presidential impeachment trial, our public life a sickening spectacle of corruption and insult with no interest in reconciliation or even integrity. There are ways to rebuild a broken world, and they require humility and empathy, a constant awareness that no one is better than anyone else. That constant awareness requires practice, vigilance, being up at all the watches.

The sages know the world is broken. They hold the broken pieces tight. An old scholar who has forgotten the Torah he studied is compared to the broken pieces of the Ten Commandments, the stone tablets that Moses smashed in frustration when the people turned to idol worship. These broken tablets were put into the Ark of the Covenant along with the new tablets that replaced them, the shattered pieces also part of the contract with God. The old scholar who has forgotten what he knew is still honored, carried by the people on their journey. Sometimes I felt like that old scholar, my memory of what I once valued fading, diminished, broken. I turned the page, and these long-dead scholars carried me along.

The comforting thing about Talmud study, and Daf Yomi in particular, is that you are never alone with it. Online, instead of people yelling at one another about why they were right, Daf Yomi learners gather to ask one another what this sentence means, whether their interpretation works, what the deeper meaning is. I am stunned by these strangers, by their sincerity and candor—qualities one rarely encounters today, online or off. To my amazement, many are non-Jews in the process of converting to Judaism, voluntarily joining this journey even in the darkness.

To my even greater amazement, one of my fellow Daf Yomi learners is my mother—the world's least pedantic person, who signed on and has shown no signs of quitting. A grandmother of fourteen, she also now recites the Sh'ma, because, as she says, "I'm up at all the watches." A mere mother of four, I'm up for many of them too. When we finish, we will be seven years older in our respective generations, and also, God willing, seven years wiser—even if we forget what we have learned, even if we are broken, even if our forgotten wisdom rattles around inside our minds like shards of broken tablets.

I still follow today's old, old news. But now I also turn away from it, toward the old, the ancient. I am forever haunted, as all living people always are, our minds the dwelling-places for the fears and hopes of those who came before us. I turn the page and return, carried by fellow readers living and dead, all turning the pages with me.

Acknowledgments

MORE THAN MOST BOOKS, THIS ONE OWES ITS LIFE TO generous editors who urged me to follow paths I might never have traveled on my own. As always, I am grateful to my agent, Gary Morris, who assured me that this project was worth pursuing, and to my Norton editor, Alane Salierno Mason, whose generosity and insight never fail to impress me.

But this time I also have many more editors to thank—those who urged me to explore topics I never considered, and also those who trusted me to follow my own questionable instincts. For their faith in the stories in this book which they were the first to publish, and also for their own brilliant ideas and suggestions, I am grateful to Alana Newhouse, David Samuels, and Matthew Fishbane of *Tablet*, Abe Socher of *Jewish Review of Books*, Jennie Rothenberg Gritz of *Smithsonian*, Rachel Dry of the *New York Times*, Marla Braverman of *Azure*, Stuart Halpern in his role as editor of the anthology *Esther in America* (Maggid Books, 2021), and Yoni Applebaum of the *Atlantic*. I am likewise indebted to the many thoughtful people who gave generously of their time to share with me their own brave and innovative approaches to understanding the Jewish past, as well as their insightful reflections on their own experiences—including Dan Ben-Canaan, Pierre Sauvage, Ala Zuskin Perelman, Jason Guberman-Pfeffer, Fran Malino, Irene Clurman, Bonnie Galat, Jean Ispa, Alex Nahumson, Jim Fry, Eddie Ashkenazie, and Chrystie Sherman, along with many others whose words did not reach these pages. And I am also grateful to those who lent me their expertise without knowing it, including the authors listed in the bibliography.

This book bears the imprint of my parents, Susan and Matthew Horn, and especially my mother, who raised me to be curious about the Jewish past and conscious of how we make use of it in the present. It also bears the influence of my husband, Brendan Schulman, who has tolerated hearing me talk about dead Jews for over twenty years, and who has always urged me to be braver than I otherwise would be.

This book is dedicated to our children, Maya, Ari, Eli, and Ronen. It is my fervent hope that they will never feel the need to read it.

Works Consulted

Alexander, Sidney. *Marc Chagall: An Intimate Biography*. New York: Paragon House, 1978.

Arendt, Hannah. *Eichmann in Jerusalem: A Report on the Banality of Evil*. New York: Viking, 1963.

Arendt, Hannah, and Mary McCarthy. *Between Friends: The Correspondence of Hannah Arendt and Mary McCarthy, 1949–1975*. Edited by Carol Brightman. New York: Harvest Books, 1996.

"As Jewish Enclaves Spring Up Around NYC, So Does Intolerance." Associated Press, January 2, 2020.

Ault, Alicia. "Did Ellis Island Officials Really Change the Names of Immigrants?" *Smithsonian*, December 2016.

Bale, Rachael, and Jani Hall. "What You Need to Know About Tiger Farms." *National Geographic*, February 2017.

Bar-Itzhak, Haya. *Jewish Poland—Legends of Origin: Ethnopoetics and Legendary Chronicles*. Detroit: Wayne State University Press, 2001.

Ben-Canaan, Dan. "The Jewish Experience in China and Harbin: The Chinese Perception of the Other." Lecture delivered at the Hong Kong Jewish Historical Society (text provided to the author). May 29, 2016.

———. *Jewish Footprints in Harbin*. Harbin: China Education Press, 2018.

———. *The Kaspe File: A Case Study of Harbin as an Intersection of Cultural and Ethnic Communities in Conflict, 1932–1945*. Harbin: Heilongjiang University People's Publishing House, 2008.

Bialik, Chaim Nachman. *Shirot Bialik: A New and Annotated Translation of Chaim Nachman Bialik's Epic Poems*. Edited and translated by Steven L. Jacobs. Columbus, Ohio: Alpha Publishing Company, 1987.

Bloom, Harold. *Shakespeare and the Invention of the Human*. New York: Riverhead, 1998.

Bowd, Stephen, and J. Donald Cullington. *"On Everyone's Lips": Humanists, Jews, and the Tale of Simon of Trent*. Phoenix: Arizona Center for Medieval and Renaissance Studies Press, 2012.

Bresler, Boris. "Harbin's Jewish Community 1898–1958: Politics, Prosperity and Adversity." *Jews of China, Volume 1: Historical and Comparative Perspectives*. Edited by Jonathan Goldstein. London: Routledge, 1998.

Caldwell, Christopher. "Hero and Oddball." Review of *A Quiet American: The Secret War of Varian Fry* by Andy Marino. *Policy Review*, February 1, 2000.

Chagall, Marc. *My Life*. 1925. Translated by Elisabeth Abbott. New York: Orion Press, 1960.

Cohen, Gerson D. "The Story of the Four Captives." *Proceedings of the American Academy for Jewish Research* 29 (1960–61).

Dautch, Aviva. "A Jewish Reading of *The Merchant of Venice*." *British Library*, March 15, 2016.

Diarna: The Geo-Museum of North African and Middle Eastern Jewish Life. Forthcoming oral-history interviews screened for the author. Publicly available archive at www.diarna.org.

Duberman, Martin. *The Worlds of Lincoln Kirstein*. New York: Knopf, 2007.

Fallon, Scott. "Tensions Within a Changing Community Are Heightened in the Wake of the Jersey City Tragedy." *The Star-Ledger* (New Jersey), December 20, 2019.

Fermaglich, Kirsten. *A Rosenberg by Any Other Name: A History of Jewish Name Changing in America*. New York: New York University Press, 2018.

Feuchtwanger, Lion. *The Oppermanns*. New York: Viking, 1934.

Frank, Anne. *Diary of Anne Frank: The Revised Critical Edition*. Edited by David Barnouw and Gerald Van Der Stroum. Netherlands Institute for War Documentation, translated by Arnold J. Pomerans et al. New York: Doubleday, 2003.

Frank, Steve. "*The Merchant of Venice* Perpetuates Vile Stereotypes of Jews." *The Washington Post*, July 28, 2016.

Fry, Varian. *Surrender on Demand*. New York: Random House, 1945.

———. Varian Fry Papers, 1940–1967. 20 boxes. Columbia University Rare Book and Manuscript Library, New York.

Gitelman, Zvi. *Jewish Nationality and Soviet Politics: The Jewish Sections of the CPSU, 1917–1930*. Princeton: Princeton University Press, 1972.

Glatshteyn, Yankev. "Good Night, World." 1938. *American Yiddish Poetry: A Bilingual Anthology*. Edited and translated by Barbara Harshav and Benjamin Harshav. Berkeley: University of California Press, 1986.

Gold, Mary Jayne. *Crossroads: Marseille, 1940*. New York: Doubleday, 1980.

Gradowski, Zalman. "The Czech Transport: Chronicle of the Auschwitz Sonderkommando." 1944. Translated by Robert Wolf. In *The Literature of Destruction: Jewish Responses to Catastrophe*, edited by David G. Roskies. Philadelphia: Jewish Publication Society, 1989.

Graetz, Heinrich. *History of the Jews, Volume 1*. Translated by Bella Lowy. Philadelphia: Jewish Publication Society, 1891.

Ibn Daud, Abraham. *The Book of Tradition: Sefer Ha-Qabbalah*. Translated by Gerson D. Cohen. Philadelphia: Jewish Publication Society, 1967.

Isenberg, Sheila. *A Hero of Our Own: The Story of Varian Fry*. New York: Random House, 2001.

Julius, Anthony. *Trials of the Diaspora*. Oxford: Oxford University Press, 2010.

Kermode, Frank. *The Sense of an Ending*. New York: Oxford University Press, 1966.

Kirstein, Lincoln. *Mosaic: Memoirs*. New York: Farrar, Straus & Giroux, 1994.

Kurshan, Ilana. *If All the Seas Were Ink*. New York: St. Martin's Press, 2017.

Lowery, Wesley, Kevin Armstrong, and Deanna Paul. "Jersey City Grapples with Ramifications of Shooting at Kosher Market." *The Washington Post*, December 12, 2019.

Marino, Andy. *A Quiet American: The Secret War of Varian Fry*. New York: St. Martin's Press, 1999.

Mendele Moykher Seforim. *The Mare*. Translated by Joachim Neugroschel. In *Great Tales of Jewish Fantasy and the Occult*, edited by Joachim Neugroschel. Woodstock, NY: Overlook Press, 1987.

Miller, Henry B. "Russian Development of Manchuria." *National Geographic*, March 1904.

Nahman of Bratslav. *Nahman of Bratslav: The Tales*. Translated by Arnold J. Band. New York: Paulist Press, 1978.

Nightingale, Carl. *Segregation: A Global History of Divided Cities*. Chicago: University of Chicago Press, 2012.

Ozick, Cynthia. "Who Owns Anne Frank?" *The New Yorker*, October 6, 1997.

Palmieri-Billig, Lisa. "Libyans Protest Jew Attempting to Reopen Synagogue." *Jerusalem Post*, October 7, 2011.

Perelman, Ala Zuskin. *The Travels of Benjamin Zuskin*. Translated by Sharon Blass. Syracuse: Syracuse University Press, 2015.

Po-chia Hsia, R. *Trent 1475: Stories of a Ritual Murder Trial*. New Haven: Yale University Press, 1996.

Rosen, Armin. "Everybody Knows: As the Leading Targets of Hate Crimes, Jews are Routinely Being Targeted in the Streets of New York City." *Tablet*, July 15, 2019.

Rosenfarb, Chava. *The Tree of Life: A Trilogy of Life in the Łódź Ghetto*. Translated by Chava Rosenfarb and Goldie Morgentaler. Madison: University of Wisconsin Press, 1985.

Rubenstein, Joshua, and Vladimir P. Naumov, eds. *Stalin's Secret Pogrom: The Postwar Inquisition of the Jewish Anti-Fascist Committee*. Translated by Laura Esther Wolfson. New Haven: Yale University Press, 2001.

Sauvage, Pierre. *And Crown Thy Good: Varian Fry and the Refugee Crisis, Marseille 1940–41*. Forthcoming film; excerpts and additional interviews screened for the author. Varian Fry Institute, Los Angeles. www.varianfry.org.

Sawin, Martica. *Surrealism in Exile and the Beginning of the New York School*. Cambridge, MA: MIT Press, 1995.

Seidman, Naomi. "Elie Wiesel and the Scandal of Jewish Rage." *Jewish Social Studies* 3, No. 1 (Autumn 1996).

Shickman-Bowman, Zvia. "The Construction of the China Eastern Railway and the Origin of the Harbin Jewish Community." *Jews of China, Volume 1: Historical and Comparative Perspectives*. Edited by Jonathan Goldstein. London: Routledge, 1998.

Sholem Aleichem. *Tevye the Dairyman and the Railroad Stories*. Translated by Hillel Halkin. New York: Schocken, 1987.

Simpich, Frederick. "Manchuria, Promised Land of Asia." *National Geographic*, October 1929.

Skidelsky, Robert. "A Chinese Homecoming." *Prospect* (UK), January 22, 2006.

Song, Lihon. "Some Observations on Chinese Jewish Studies." *Contemporary Jewry* 29, No. 3 (December 2009).

Su, Ling. "Harbin Jews: The Truth." *Southern Metropolis Life Weekly* (China), April 2007.

The Travels of Benjamin of Tudela. Animated film (non-credited), 1978. Oster Visual Documentation Center, Museum of the Jewish People (Beit Hatfutsot), Tel Aviv.

U.S. Millennial Holocaust Knowledge and Awareness Survey. Survey commissioned by Claims Conference (Conference on Jewish Material Claims Against Germany) and conducted by Schoen Consulting, www .claimscon.org, 2020.

Weisz, George, and Donatella Lippi. "Roderigo Lopez: Physician-in-Chief to Queen Elizabeth I of England." *Rambam Medical Journal* 8, No. 3 (July 2017).

White, Nic. "Anne Frank House Banned Orthodox Jewish Employee from Wearing His Skullcap at Work." *Daily Mail* (UK), April 15, 2018.

Yehoshua, A. B. *Mr. Mani*, 1989. Translated by Hillel Halkin. New York: Doubleday, 1992.

Praise for *Eternal Life*

"Riveting, startling, hilarious, and sad—I've never read anything like it."

—Elif Batuman, author of *The Idiot*

"[*Eternal Life*] shimmers with Horn's signature blend of tragedy and spirituality."

—Ron Charles, *Washington Post*

"The question at the heart of this wise and appealing novel is finally not how Rachel finds meaning in her eternal life. It is how we, despite our portions of sorrow, tedium and disaster, persist in finding meaning in ours."

—Joshua Max Feldman, *New York Times Book Review*

"Masterful. . . . *Eternal Life* is at its core a serious meditation on the meaning of life and purpose of death."

—Renee Ghert-Zand, *Times of Israel*

"The chilling pathos of Dara Horn's *Eternal Life* is bound to turn every mortal reader into a philosopher of cosmic joy."

—Cynthia Ozick, author of *Antiquities*

Praise for *A Guide for the Perplexed*

"Horn frames a contest between predetermination and free will in which her characters are each humbled, a religious dialogue taking the form of this humane, erudite novel."

—Saul Austerlitz, *Boston Globe*

"Riveting. . . . This is extraordinary material, emotionally resonant and intellectually suggestive. . . . Beautifully written."

—Wendy Smith, *Washington Post*

"[An] intense, multilayered story. . . . [Horn's] writing comes from a place of deep knowledge."

—Jami Attenberg, *New York Times Book Review*

"I really urge you to read Dara Horn."

—Bill Goldstein, NBC *Today Show*

"Intricate and suspenseful, *A Guide for the Perplexed* is both learned and heartfelt, an exploration of human memory, its uses and misuses, that spans centuries in a twisty braid full of jaw-dropping revelations and breathtaking reversals. An elegant and brainy page-turner from a master storyteller."

—Geraldine Brooks, Pulitzer Prize winner and
author of *The Secret Chord*

"Computer science and medieval philosophy mesh in Dara Horn's accomplished novel about digital dangers and the nature of memory."

—Barbara Kiser, *Nature*

"Wondrous. . . . [A] novelist at the height of her powers."

—Andrew Furman, *Miami Herald*

Praise for *All Other Nights*

Booklist **25 Best Books of the Decade**
Book-of-the-Month Club Selection
ABA Indie Book Sense Pick
New York Times Book Review **Editors' Choice**

"Slam-bang . . . superb . . . a gripping plot premise and a fascinatingly conflicted protagonist. . . . [A] marvelous variety of characters, each imagined with empathy and depth."

—Wendy Smith, *Washington Post*

"Welcome to Dara Horn's stellar third novel. . . . *All Other Nights* has the propulsive, suspenseful narrative of an espionage thriller, [and] the larger moral dilemmas Horn weaves into an epic."

—Sarah Weinman, *New York Post*

"A tale of adventure . . . betrayal and love, dignity and loss, that takes the breath away and makes the heart pound."

—Anne Roiphe, author of *Ballad of the Black and Blue Mind*

"An enjoyably fast-paced amalgam of historical romance, spy novel and political thriller . . . rare and memorable."

—Emily Bingham, *Wall Street Journal*

"Engrossing. . . . [D]elicious."

—Rebecca Tuhus-Dubrow, *New York Times Book Review*

Praise for *The World to Come*

"Isn't there a Willy Wonka gum that tastes like all good foods at once? If so, Dara Horn's *The World to Come* is the literary equivalent of that confection. . . . [E]ach page of her novel is a marvel."

—Debra Spark, *San Francisco Chronicle*

"Horn's deft touch is often wryly funny—but never maliciously so. . . . An accomplished work that beautifully explains how families—in all their maddening, smothering, supportive glory—create us."

—Natalie Danford, *Los Angeles Times Book Review*

"Deeply sympathetic characters, an encyclopedic grasp of 20th-century history and a spiritual sense that sees through the conventional barriers between this life and the one to come—or the one before."

—Ron Charles, *Washington Post*

"Symphonic and piercingly beautiful. . . . [T]he novel suspends us between emotions, never allowing any to become predominant, and we hang there in that indeterminate space, perfectly happy, hoping that the book will never end."

—Bethany Schneider, *Newsday*

"A deeply satisfying literary mystery and a funny-sad meditation on how the past haunts the present—and how we haunt the future."

—Lev Grossman, *Time*

Praise for *In the Image*

Winner of the National Jewish Book Award
Winner of the Reform Judaism Prize for
Jewish Fiction
Winner of the Edward Lewis Wallant Award

"Powerful . . . *In the Image* not only underscores Jewish identity in America, but more universally, gives suffering meaning and, in the end, hope."

—*Seattle Times*

"[An] unsettling, otherworldly novel."

—*Boston Globe*

"Told with moral passion, vigor, humor, and an unflagging fascination with the coincidences, miseries, grotesqueries, and triumphs of life."

—Richard Snow, *American Heritage*

"Incredibly poignant . . . with audacious appropriation of lines and themes from Jewish texts. . . . It takes a writer with great self-confidence to pull off this sort of work. . . . [Horn is] a true talent."

—*Jerusalem Post*

"Richly imagined. . . . [An] intricate web of miracles, coincidences and accidents of fate."

—*New York Times Book Review*

"*In the Image* is not merely a striking success as a whole but a technical tour de force [that] has a strange, compelling, romantic fascination."

—David Gelernter, *Commentary*